Make Money Online:

I0478449

How I Make $3000+ A Month

Kiera Jennings

CONTENTS

MY BONUS FOR YOU – MY BOOK
ON ACHIEVING SUCCESS IN LIFE
Think Your Way to Success

Introduction

So, you want to make money online. I've been earning my living online for many years, and have looked into all kinds of options to do so. So far, my highest income for one month (from online sources only) was $6500. Of that, $4000 was just from online publishing (book sales). I'm not going to tell you that making money online is easy, but it is definitely possible. While I wouldn't suggest quitting your job to pursue this, it is a great option to start making money on the side and grow it from there. That's what I did.

I know many people need to make money NOW. Many methods to make money online take a while. If you write a book and publish it on Kindle Direct Publishing, you'll have to wait at least two months to be paid as the payments are lagged by that amount of time. If you build a website to monetize with Adsense, it takes months, if not longer, to see any real money. You need traffic to your site, which is easier said than done. Same thing with a blog. There is a lot of upfront work before it starts to make any money at all. So, if you're in the kind of situation where you need money now to buy some groceries or keep the roof over your head, I would try Textbroker. Let's start there...

Textbroker

Textbroker is a website (textbroker.com) that hires writers (authors they call them) to write articles for individuals and companies who post orders on their site. If you have any writing ability, you should be able to make money doing this. Writers are rated 2 star, 3 star (average), 4 star (like me) and 5 star. The higher your star rating, the more you are paid per word, and thus per article. At three stars, you make a penny a word. You'll be paid $5.00 for a 500 word article. At 4 stars, I make 1.4 cents per word, so for a 1000 word article, I make $14.00. When I first started out on Textbroker, I was a 3 star rating but was recently moved up to 4 stars, probably because of the current demand for articles.

Once you are approved, you gain access to assignments that are available for your star rating. You click on Assignments and then on Show Orders to start looking at what's available. Right now, there are 5,202 articles waiting for people to write them (I just checked the site now). Lots of work is waiting right there.

You click on an article that you might want to write and then it gives the specifics of that particular assignment. You are then given 10 minutes to read it over and decide if you want to do it. If not, you can just go back to the Orders and look at another one. The nice thing is that during that 10 minutes, no one else can take the order. Also, you are only allowed one article at a time – you usually have 24 hours to write and submit it (depending on the article – some give you three days or more), then you can pick another assignment. If you write and submit the article in half an hour, you can immediately grab another assignment. I like this because it means writers can't hog all the articles – everyone can only work on one assignment at a time.

How to Pick Them

When you read over the assignments, pick ones that seem simple. The faster you can complete acceptable articles, the more money you will make. If an assignment seems like it requires too much research or a long list of instructions, you don't want it. Go on to the next. I pick articles that I could write with little to no research at all. I also take assignments where the instructions are SHORT. The shorter, the better. If the person requesting the article wrote up a huge descriptions of what they want, or worse, wants you to look at a google docs document outlining the requirements for it, skip it. Chances are, you won't be able to satisfy them (they are picky) and if you were able to please them, it would take entirely too long.

Articles seem to be renewed weekly, as sometimes I will look at orders and there will be only a few hundred, but then I will check the next day and there will be 6,000 of them.

How You Get Paid

Articles are accepted by the people who ordered them or, if it takes them too long, they are automatically accepted by the Textbroker system within a couple of days (I believe 48 hours). To get a payout, you need to have at least $10 in your account. You can request a payout at any time. Payouts requested by 11:59 on Thursdays will be paid on Friday.

This means you should start early in the week. Do as many assignments as you can so that the money shows up in your account in time to request a Thursday pay-out (by midnight) – and you'll be paid on Friday!

If you do a couple of easy articles per day, which should take you no more than an hour or so, you will make between $300 – 500 per month depending on whether you get a 3 star or 4 star ranking. If you lose your job or don't have a current job and work at it full-time, you will obviously make a whole lot more.

I prefer Textbroker over some sites like Upwork (formerly Elance) because you don't have to waste any time bidding on jobs or waiting for customers. The work is right there for the taking, so you can spend time making money instead of looking for work. I've done work for Textbroker since 2011 – and believe me – it's better than ever. They have a lot more articles than they did six years ago. The articles available to write used to max out in the hundreds – now it's in the thousands! Unlike some websites that were not able to get the customers to stay in business, Textbroker is thriving! Now, let's talk about another site where people are making a lot of money…

What's Fiverr?

Fiverr is truly the Ebay of services - in fact they call themselves the world's largest marketplace for small services. People who use the Fiverr.com website do so for a variety of reasons: 86% want to be their own boss and have independence, 72% want to increase the amount of money they make each month, 40% want more fun and excitement, while 32% say they want to get more experience. I realize these don't add up to 100% - the users were able to choose more than one reason that they use Fiverr. However, this gives you an idea of the variety of reasons that people use the site, but most do it for the extra monthly income. Yay!

People offer the services they know how to perform as well as their talents on the site. According to Fiverr, over 15% of users have made over $1000 on the site. Granted, this doesn't sound like a large percentage but that is due to the fact that many people who put gigs up on Fiverr just aren't serious about making money. They haven't spent time researching what gigs to offer, and they aren't willing to work on Fiverr on a daily basis. There are 27% that have made over $500, however there are some sellers who make well over $2000 a month from Fiverr gigs. Truthfully, the more you want to work, the more money you'll make. If you're willing to work, you can definitely make a lot of money on Fiverr.

There is a catch, though. You have to know which gigs to offer. Some gigs do amazingly well, with sellers having 15 customer orders in queue (lined up). Other gigs don't get purchased, and the seller can go forever without a single sale. So, we're going to spend a lot of time going over how to find gigs that do the best in terms of sales and also how to find the kinds of gigs you should offer. Many people use trial and error to see what works and what doesn't. However, reading this book can save you a lot of time on this step - and time is money after all.

Most gigs on Fiverr cost $5, of which the seller receives $4 and the Fiverr site gets $1 per gig. However, because higher level sellers can offer services that are called GigExtras for higher amounts of money ($10, $20), 36% of gigs sell for over $5. Even more exciting is the fact that 14% of the site's users use Fiverr as their main source of income.

What do people do with their Fiverr earnings? Well, that has been studied as well. Almost an equal percentage of sellers save their earnings and use it to assist in paying their regular expenses (40%, 39%). Interestingly, 35% use the money they make on Fiverr to build a business, either one on Fiverr or a different business. That's what I did - I used Fiverr to build up funds to start my publishing company. We'll discuss more on that later.

Categories on Fiverr

Sellers on Fiverr offer services such as Web Development, Business Translation, Personalized Greetings, Graphic Design, Writing, Advertising, Marketing, and so on. There are currently nine main categories with numerous subcategories under those. Let's take a brief look at each of the main ones.

Advertising includes things such as human billboards, radio, flyers and handouts, banner advertising and music promotion, among others.

Writing and Translation includes copywriting, SEO keyword optimization, creative writing and scripting, translation, reviews, resumes and cover letters, editing, press releases, and speech writing.

Video and Animation includes commercials, editing and post production, animation, and testimonials by actors. Again, many other things are included under this category.

Graphics & Design has cartoons and caricatures, logo design, illustration, ebook covers and packages, web design, photoshopping, flyers and brochues, business cards - you name it.

Digital Marketing includes social media, SEO, Web Traffic, Email Marketing, etc.

Business includes business plans, career advice, market research, virtual assistants, market research, branding, legal consulting, and financial consulting.

Programming and Tech has .Net, HTML, CSS, Wordpress, Java, Databases, Javascript, and so on.

Music and Audio includes Audio Editing and Mastering, Jingles, Songwriting, Music Lessons, Narration and voiceovers, custom ringtones, and more.

Fun and Lifestyle contains Celebrity Impersonators, Daredevils, Your Message On, Pranks, Dancers, animal care and pets, relationship advice, diet and weight loss, health and fitness, astrology, cooking recipes, spirituality, parenting, travel, etc.

There are some seriously bizarre gigs on Fiverr, so you are forewarned that once you start surfing the site it is hard to get off of it. Some of the more bizarre gigs involve dressing up as a chicken or other character, having someone pretend to be your girlfriend on Facebook for a period of time, or painting the name of your website on a part of the seller's body. Basically, if you can think it up, chances are someone is either offering that service or one that resembles it.

You can click on the Fiverr Gig Categories at the bottom of the Fiverr.com homepage to get a complete listing of all categories and their contents. This should give you lots of ideas of the kinds of things that can be offered for sale on the site.

How Fiverr Works

Here are the steps for selling on Fiverr, according to the website:

Create a gig for a service you are willing to offer, then share your gig with the world, you will be notified when your gig is ordered, your account will be credited $4 forty-eight hours after you deliver the work (you get $4 for every $5 a customer pays) , and you can withdraw your money once its available (usually 14 days is the clearing period). (Fiverr.com) Basically, for every $5 a buyer pays, you get $4 and fiverr gets $1.

You now have the ability as a seller to set up three packages – what you'll do for your customer and for what price. Be sure to set up all packages on all your gigs to maximize the amount of money you make. You can also set up Gig Extras – where you will do something extra for a fee. For example, for an extra $10 you might offer to finish the project within 24 hours.

You need a Paypal account to get paid by Fiverr, so work on getting one of those if you don't already have one. Then, you register for Fiverr, which is self-explanatory - your information plus your paypal address so they can pay you. The only other withdrawal provider is a Fiverr Revenue Card, which is a Mastercard where your Fiverr funds can be placed. There are fees associated with both Paypal and Fiverr Revenue Card, so check out the Terms of Service on the site to see which you would prefer.

Once your registration goes through, you can start listing gigs. That's what each service you will offer is called. Fiverr allows you to list 20 gigs and the best part is - your listings are FREE. So, really, why wouldn't you register and put up some gigs in order to make some extra money. Obviously, we want to maximize our earnings, so we will list all 20 gigs (once we decide what we're going to offer).

You can do Gig videos to talk directly to your customers as opposed to just having customers read your gig on the site. Gig videos are normally more successful than gigs where the seller does not do a video, so taking the time to do videos for your gigs should pay off.

At first, you will only be a Level 1 seller. You can click on your user name at the top right of the main page of fiverr once you register. Click on Selling and Create a Gig. Fill in the information relevant to your gig - it asks you all the info it requires so this is pretty easy as well. You will need a category, a description, instructions for your customer, an image (picture), tags (keywords that describe your gig), and your maximum number of days to complete. You can make up your packages. Hit Save at the bottom when you're done. As soon as your gig is approved by Fiverr, it will be listed in their search.

Also, remember that your 20 gigs **can not** be duplicates - they have to be a little different from each other or they will be denied by Fiverr. So, you can come up with different versions or variations on what you will do for each of your gigs.

A Word About SEO

In order for your gig to come up high in the search results on the site, you need to put the keywords related to your gig as close to the beginning of the title of the gig as possible. So, for an article writing gig, it would be good to title it "I will write an article that is SEO in less than 24 hours for $5". Notice I put 'write an article' at the beginning of the title of the gig - not the end.

The same goes for the description you write for your gig - put your main keywords (those that describe your gig the best and that people are likely to use as search terms for a gig like yours) in the first sentence of the description. Fiverr will not allow you to submit a gig if you use the same word over and over, so just use each different keyword a couple of times. If it won't allow you to submit, just remove the word that it is saying is being used too much and use a different word until it is happy and let's you submit.

Also, use keywords in your tags. You are allowed to tag your gig with keywords when you create each new gig. So, pick keywords that people would use to search for a gig like yours. For an article writing gig, you might use tags such as article, write, articles, SEO, words, unique, writer, etc.

Your Account

You have a Profile that includes settings and your collections. Under settings is information about you such as your user name and a brief statement about yourself, if you like. If you will mostly be doing one kind of gig, like writing, you could pick a user name related to the gig, like Sallywriter. If you believe you will be doing a mixture of different types of gigs (with 20 that is pretty likely) then just pick a generic user name you like. Obviously, pick something that is customer friendly - we want to attract customers, not turn them off.

The Favorites part of your account profile is made up of all the gigs you saw and you "collected" because you found them interesting. I use this to collect gigs I think are doing well and that I could either do or could learn to do. To add something to your favorites, hit the "Favorite" button at the top of the gig page (once you have clicked on a gig and are on the main gig page for that particular gig).

To purchase a gig, a buyer simply clicks on Buy and the money is taken out of either their Fiverr account (if they have funds in their currently) or they are then directed to pay via Paypal. Then, the buyer is given the buyer instructions that you put in for your gig. For example, if the seller was going to review a product for you, you would have to provide a link for the product perhaps. Once the buyer sends the buyer instructions back, the clock begins to tick. The seller now has the period of time that they set on the gig to complete and deliver the gig (via the Fiverr site). So, if I say it will take me 3 days to do a gig, I have three days from the time that the buyer submits the info I requested of them (such as a link).

Ratings

One thing I really like about Fiverr is their rating system - buyers are automatically asked to provide a rating for the seller upon delivery of a gig and the rating is either positive or negative (one or another). This simple rating system works out to be fairer than any other system I've seen. By delivering what you promised on time, you can maintain a 100% positive rating for a long time. I know, because I have a 100% positive rating after being on the site for more than a year.

Getting Paid

One big drawback I feel Fiverr has is that it takes a while to get paid - it takes 14 days for a payment to clear and end up available for withdrawal. At that point, you can withdraw your money to your Paypal account or to a Fiverr Revenue Card. This is a bummer at first, however, once you start to do gigs every day, you will constantly have money clearing. It is best to let it accumulate to $50 or more prior to withdrawing so that you do not incur lots of fees (as mentioned, Paypal and the Fiverr Revenue Card do have associated fees). Right now, Paypal is a 2% fee on the amount of money being withdrawn.

Terms of Service

First of all, I would read the Terms of Service all the way through. I know - really boring, but keeping your account in good standing is absolutely essential to making money through Fiverr. If you get banned, you will not be able to make any money. So, learn the rules and stick by them. They are usually pretty reasonable about giving warnings and just denying gigs that they think are duplicates or not appropriate or allowed. But, be safe and know the rules so you can stay out of trouble.

Fiverr Seller Levels

You start out as a Level 1 Seller. According to Fiverr, this is Level 1:

"You've been active on the site for 30 days and completed at least 10 orders while maintaining excellent ratings and a great track record. You'll automatically be promoted to Level 1. At this Level, you'll gain additional features making it easier for you to offer more advanced services and generate a higher income." (Fiverr.com)

Level 2

"You made over 50 orders in the past two months while maintaining excellent ratings and a solid track record. You'll automatically be promoted to Level 2, unlocking advanced sales tools to further expand your services and increase your sales. You'll also receive priority support." (Fiverr.com)

Top Rated Seller

"Top Rated Sellers are manually chosen by Fiverr editors. Promotion is based on criteria including: seniority, volume of sales, extremely high rating, exceptional customer care and community leadership. As a Top Rated Seller, you'll gain access to more extensive sales tools, early access to beta features and VIP support." (Fiverr.com)

I am currently a Level 2 Seller. I have noticed that the more active you are on the site, the higher you will show up in their search engine. So, it is really important to stay active on the site as much as possible. I will also say that my earnings really shot up once I became a Level 2 Seller, which only took about a month. That is something to definitely shoot for.

To move up in Levels, you should do the following, according to Fiverr:

- Receive positive reviews regularly

- Always deliver on time

- Invest in self promotion

- Communicate quickly and politely

- Stay out of trouble, follow the rules

Making $200 per month is pretty easy on Fiverr, and many users say they make $200 to $300 a month. At a net income of $4 per gig, that's only 50 gigs in a month or a little over one per day. To get up to $500 plus level, you have to be a bit more savvy. You can't just offer any gig - you have to offer a popular gig. You want to offer several gigs that will have 5 or more customers queued up in each (that means they have ordered and paid and are in line for you to complete their order). The great thing about finding a popular gig is that you can surf the site to find popular gigs you can do or you can learn to do. Once you find a gig that is showing several people in queue (which is listed right up near the top of the gig description), you should collect it in your Favorites by clicking on "Favorite" under the gig Title.

Much like Ebay, you can't just decide you're going to sell crocheted headbands and make a forture. Or, for a service example, you can't just want to offer a gig where you sing Happy Birthday dressed up as a duck. First, we need to research to find out if this is something that customers on Fiverr really want. Once we know what gigs they want, it is simply a means of offering those gigs. If you don't know how to provide that service, a quick search on the internet should give you some instruction on how to perform that task.

Because Fiverr allows you to list 20 gigs at no cost to you, we obviously want to post the maximum number of gigs so that we get plenty of exposure and can offer a variety of services. So, find 20 super popular gigs that you either know how to do or can learn relatively easily. How do we find these super popular gigs? Look on Fiverr - do research on the site.

Researching Gigs

Here's how to do the research. Type something into the search engine on the Fiverr site (at the top of the page). Next, you will see that at the side of the results there are a number of ways to sort the results. These sorting methods you can choose are by category, by sellers who are currently online, by how fast an order can be completed, by seller level, by the price, etc.

In your search results, fiverr will show you the highest rated sellers offering that kind of gig (whatever you typed into the search) and also the most active sellers offering this type of gig. Start clicking on the top listed ones, and you will likely find that they have many sales in queue (if it is a popular gig). Once you find a popular gig, collect it so you have it to refer back to when coming up with your own super popular gigs.

You can also tell how popular a gig is by looking at how old the gig is and how many positive reviews it has gotten. Check out the reviews - they are dated so you can actually count how many gigs were sold via a 7 day period, a month, and so on. So, we are using this information to find gigs that sell regularly. Not all sellers have to leave a rating of positive or negative, so the actual sales figure could be higher, however this does give us a good way to gauge the amount of sales.

OK - so I just did this search process and the first listing is for a gig created 4 months ago that has over 200 positive reviews. So, this guy made at least $800 (200 gigs times $4 each) in 4 months, or $200 per month on just this one gig of his.

He currently has six orders that he's working on (in queue), and he offers express 24 hour delivery. So, this is a very active gig. Also, he has 100% positive rating and is a Level 2 seller. There are GigExtras listed on the gig, so he is actually making more than the $4 we used in our figure above. Also, because not all customers leave reviews of the seller, he has actually had more customers than the 200 we used in our figure above. So, we know our estimate of what he makes is a bit low, but it still tells us that this is a money maker. Simple.

Fiverr Favorites

Click Favorite, and keep searching. Again, we need a minimum of 20 very popular gigs that you can offer for sale. Do your research - the time you spend up front will pay off in spades later on. There's no sense in offering some 'shot in the dark' gigs when there is a very easy way to figure out what sells, what makes money. Be smart and don't waste your time creating gigs that no one is willing to pay for. Put all the great gigs you find in your Favorites. Those are the ones you're going to copy - not word for word of course - change the wording a bit so you don't get in any trouble when you go to post the gigs. Same thing with the gig descriptions - rewrite them in your own words. Don't use their descriptions word for word or you could get snagged for doing that. Change them around, change words, make the gig your own.

Once you pick your money-making gigs, simply post them. It may take a day or so for them to show up in the search results so it will be slow at first. Also, the higher your seller level, the higher you will show up in the search results - as well as the more active you are. So, its very important to get sales and deliver great customer service to get to a Level 2 within a month. This is definitely possible - I did it in that amount of time.

When I first started on Fiverr, I worked like a crazy person. I offered all 24 hour express orders so that I could beat out my competitors and get as many customers in as short a time as possible. That's how I got to Level 2 so fast. By the time I reached Level 2, I was getting a bit worn out so I switched over to offering 24 hour service as a GigExtra instead. I added GigExtras, and immediately made more money per sale (at the time I started, you had to be a Level 2 to offer GigExtras). So, I was making more money per sale and had more time to deliver my gigs to customers. Things were definitely getting easier.

I spent time researching gigs that sell, and added gigs until I had all 20 being offered. I have sold copywriting in the form of articles, I have reviewed people's resumes, and I've created an informational report that I've sold on Fiverr. There are many ways to make money if you are willing to do the work.

I was selling up to six gigs per day, and none of them took me that much time. One secret to gigs is that you not only want ones that sell well, but you also want ones that you can perform quickly. If you can do a gig in ten minutes, then you are making the equivalent of $24 per hour ($4 for ten minutes would equal $24 per hour). When choosing the gigs you will offer, keep in mind that the faster you can do the gig, the more money you will make in less time.

If you set aside an hour each night, from 7 to 8, for example, you could do the gigs you have sold for the day during that time period. Fiverr does a great job of letting you know how much time you have left before you have to deliver a gig. Make sure you deliver your gigs on time! Awesome customer service is key.

Once my gigs were averaging $8 each, just doing 2 per day would give me $480 per month. That's how you start making money on Fiverr. Some people think you can't make money selling $4 gigs, but once you get going, you can make a lot of extra money each month. Remember, we are selling packages and GigExtras as well. You can also do it right at home, on your own schedule. It sure beats having to get a part-time job and drive to it every day. You can stay at home, make dinner, be with your family, and even fulfill your gigs while watching TV at night. It really is a great system.

You also have a Buyer tab at the top of your page, where you can keep track of what you've bought in My Shopping and also Payments. Fiverr is great for purchasing services you need for very little money. Many of us have numerous business ventures, and you'll likely find during your research on the site many services you'd like to purchase as well. I have bought Kindle ebook covers, Kindle conversion services, articles, and so on from other sellers on Fiverr. They are a great resource for an entrepreneur. You can even use the money you've made that's in your Fiverr account (once it clears) to purchase services on Fiverr.

Naturally, check out a seller's rating prior to purchasing from them. If they have a positive rating and lots of positive reviews, then you are pretty safe purchasing from them.

The Inbox takes you to your Fiverr mail system where you can communicate with buyers and sellers on Fiverr. Another great option is the button at the top right of each gig that allows you to contact the seller. You can ask a question or if they could provide a service that is a little different that what they've advertised, etc. Because professional Fiverr sellers are super with customer service, you can expect a reply in 24 hours or less.

At the top of your page is your Dashboard, Inbox, Notifications, and Shopping Cart. Take some time to look around at all the services that Fiverr offers to sellers and buyers.

Marketing Your Gigs

Fiverr is set up so that you can click a button and share your gig on Facebook or on Twitter. Once you get a higher seller status, you can also simply click a button to share your new status with your Twitter followers or Facebook friends. So, they make it easy to advertise your gigs as well using different social media. You should, of course, do this as more exposure means more sales.

The Game Plan

First of all, you need to get a Paypal account if you don't already have one. Go to Paypal.com and sign up for an account. You will have to verify your account, which is usually done by Paypal sending a few cents into your account, you look up what was deposited by Paypal, and then you go onto your account and say how much was deposited in your account. This is done in order to verify this is really your bank account. This takes a few days, obviously, so sign up for your Paypal account first.

Sign up with Fiverr.com for your own account once you have a Paypal account. Go through the registration process we discussed. Read the Terms of Service so that you know the rules and don't do anything to get your account banned. Now, it's time to research money-making gigs. Let's move on to that at this point.

Now, I'm going to walk you through the research process. What we are trying to do at this time is find super-popular gigs that are selling a lot so we know what kind of gigs to post ourselves.

Go to Fiverr.com. Under the logo and picture, you will see where you can search for gigs. Click on the filter to find Level 2 sellers in that category. That's our best chance to see people under this search term that are doing well on Fiverr.

Right now, I click on the first one. The woman is offering to send 2500 followers to your twitter account and then tweet your message out to a million people. There are 9 orders in queue (meaning she is currently working on 9 orders that have been placed). That's a good sign - orders in queue mean the seller is busy. She has a 100% rating, and its an express gig, which means that she delivers the order within 24 hours.

She has 2548 positive views, which means in the 7 months since the gig was created (info right up under the title of the gig). We know she makes at least $4 per gig, but is probably making a lot more as she is a Level 2 seller. So, worst case scenario, she has made $10,192 on this ONE GIG so far (in 7 months). If you'd like to see how much she's made in the last week, simply count the number of reviews she received during the last seven days (they are all dated). Again, not everyone leaves a review, so the number is probably higher. I suspect, from my own experience, that she is making twice that amount (closer to $20,000) because I know my average sale went up from $4 to about $8 once I got my level 2. Anyway, this woman is making about $1500 a month, minimum on just this one gig. Remember, we get to list 20 gigs, not just one.

Now granted, you may not know how to (or even want to) give twitter followers to other people or tweet out messages to your twitter followers. In fact, some things people offer are questionable and may violate the terms of an external site (such as Twitter) so you have to make sure you can find something that won't get you in trouble or get any of your accounts (like Fiverr, Twitter, Amazon) banned. It's a personal decision what you are willing to do and what you are not - not my decision to make. Remember, right now we are just researching.

The next gig listed is one for SEO. This guy is willing to create 50 edu backlinks plus 200 PR 1 to PR 6 from High Authority Wiki Sites. He has had over 15, 600 sales. He has 35 orders in queue. He has over 9,000 positive reviews. Is he making money? You bet.

Continue working your way down the gigs, and click the Favorite button whenever you find a super popular gig you might be able to offer or offer a version of. We are researching information on what gigs really sell because those are the kind we want to offer.

Now, say you have an idea of what you want to offer. If you're a writer and want to offer something related to that, you can put in a term such as 'article writing' (in the search at the top of the page) and then click on the Level 2 Seller filter and get the results.

The first gig that comes up has more to do with SEO than actual article writing, so we'll skip that one. The top article writing gig is a woman offering a 400 word High Quality SEO Article in 2 days or its Free. She has 39 orders in queue, and she says on the gig that she's sold over $55,000 worth of articles. This gig was created a year ago, and she offers express delivery for an extra $5. Is she busy? Is she making lots of money? Yes and yes.

Writing a 400 word article in two days is something pretty much anyone can do - I can do about 3 an hour. SEO stands for search engine optimization, meaning keywords are used in the article title, beginning of the article, and throughout so that search engines will find the article when someone search for an article on that subject. Many, many site owners need lots of fresh SEO articles written constantly, so this should be a revenue source for a long, long time. If you'd like to learn how to write an SEO article, look it up on the internet. Learn a skill, and you too can offer this gig to Fiverr customers.

Kindle services are very popular right now. People need covers created, conversions done for Createspace paperbacks, audio books, and so on. Some people on Fiverr even offer to upload your ebook to your Amazon account for you. I don't use this service as uploading is pretty easy, but it is still a service that's offered. Some gigs are editing gigs, so they will edit your ebook for you. Anyway, if you're thinking of doing something related to kindle, just type that into the search. You will be able to see which Kindle gigs are selling. Again, don't do anything that will violate the terms of service of amazon if you are doing Kindle gigs or you could lose your account.

So, I typed kindle into the search box on Fiverr. The first gig that comes up is one that creates ebook covers for people. The guy has 30 orders in queue, so he is pretty busy. He has just under 2,000 positive reviews and created this gig 8 months ago. His last review was posted just 3 hours ago, and the second to last was posted 8 hours ago. So, he is very busy, working like crazy, and making lots of money. He is offering GigExtras for $5 each, including express delivery in one day and also finding a photo for your cover.

Hopefully by now you have a good idea on how to find what's popular and what's selling on Fiverr. Favorite the ones that are of interest to you so that you can design your 20 gigs around these same sorts of things. We want only winning gigs in our arsenal.

If you have a specific idea for a gig, try and look it up on the Fiverr site. Are there any gigs that show up in a search for the gig you'd like to try offering? Did anyone ever purchase that gig? How many reviews are listed? Compare that to the time period that the gig was created in. For example, if you come up with a gig and find a similar one (by doing a search on Fiverr) that has 6 reviews listed and the gig was created six months ago, you know this isn't the way to go. One sale a month at $4 or so will not cut it...

So, research first and design your gigs based upon what you've found in your research. If you don't know how to perform a gig like the popular one you found, do a little research on the computer to see if you can find out how hard it is to perform that gig and if there are directions or training available on how to do it. Even if you had to invest $20 on a book on how to write SEO articles, for example, that would be a good investment in your article writing business on Fiverr.

Time is money, so don't waste time coming up with gigs off the top of your head and listing them, only to find out that they won't sell. That's not a smart use of your time. Research first, design your gigs, learn how to do them if necessary, and then post them.

The next step is outperforming your Fiverr competition. To get lots of sales and move up to a Level 2 Seller, you need to beat them out. So, over-offer at first. If they are offering their gig with a 3 day delivery, offer it in 24 hours instead. Look at what they are offering their gig customers, and trump them by offering just a little bit more than they are. Getting lots of sales to move up to a Level 2 seller is absolutely essential to our game plan. We need the extra exposure in the search engine that an active Level 2 seller receives. More exposure equals more sales.

Now that you're underway as a Level 2 seller, remember to go back and tweak your gigs. Are some selling better than others? Why? Can you change them? If some aren't selling, find a different gig to offer that will be successful. We want all 20 of our gigs to be bringing in orders. When you add GigExtras, think of what extras a customer would want. What would they pay an extra $20 for? What would they pay an extra $10 for? What about an extra $5? Sometimes, sellers use the GigExtras to offer express service - some people don't want to wait in line and will pay extra to 'cut in line' so to speak. So, continually adjust your gigs so you are making the maximum amount you can from each of your 20 gigs.

Again, it takes 14 days for the money to clear and be available for withdrawal. Keep in mind, however, once you are doing gigs daily you will also have money clearing each and every day (after the intial 14 days wait for that first payment to clear). Remember, it is better to let the money build up a little (like to $50 or $100) as there are fees associated with Paypal and loading your Fiverr card, if you have one.

Remember to treat your Fiverr business like a business - you will have to pay taxes on that income you make on Fiverr, of course, but you should also take it as seriously as you would a real job. Here are some techniques for treating Fiverr like a business.

Check Fiverr several times a day to see if you have orders or if any customers or potential customers have asked you any questions on your Fiverr account. You need to be very vigilant in answering questions - exceptional customer service is rare today, and if you offer it to your customers, they will show you with praise in your reviews, which cause even more people to buy your gigs.

Set aside a particular time of day when you will do your Fiverr gigs - it can be whenever you have time. I do Fiverr gigs at night around 7 o'clock while I'm watching television. It's fun to know I'm making money while watching TV with my kids. If you have time available in the morning, set aside time then to do your gigs. It's really up to you and your schedule. Just make it a habit so that you don't forget your gig orders, which will result in negative reviews. Also, if you don't deliver on time, Fiverr gives the buyer the option to cancel the sale.

Communicate a lot with your customers. I always keep them up-to-date on their order. I message them that I've received their order and am working on it. Just don't make promises you can't keep - its better to say on a gig that you need 3 days to complete and deliver in one day than to do the opposite. Remember that we want to over-deliver.

I also send a note when I deliver a gig that says they should contact me if there are any issues or need any changes. I want to make sure I keep my 100% positive rating - there's no faster way to lose customers than for your rating to drop and bad reviews to show on your gig. Your business depends on a flawless rating and plenty of stellar reviews for potential customers to read before deciding to order.

Give it some time - it will take a little while for your gigs to gain rank in the search on Fiverr, and you need your Level 2 to really start pulling in lots of sales and higher value sales. The good news is that you will be making extra money - perhaps only $100 to $200 your first month, but that will definitely increase if you follow the advice laid out in this ebook. Every little bit helps, right? That'll be a couple hundred more than you made last month.

Because we know that we will get a minimum of $4 per sale, you can figure out how many gigs you need to sell and perform in order to reach your revenue goal. Say you want to make $1000 a month on Fiverr. Once you reach a Level 2 seller status, you should average about $8 per sale when taking into account your GigExtras. So, $1000 divided by $8 is 125 sales needed for the month. Given that most months have 31 days, we need just 4 gigs sold per day to reach your goal.

Now, let's say you are just a Level 1 seller - what you'll start out at. At an average of $4 per gig, you would need to sell 250 to make $1000 a month. This works out to about 8 sales per day. Definitely doable when we see how many orders are in queue for some of the popular gigs being offered. It won't happen overnight, but you'll be surprised how quickly your sales will increase as you fill more and more orders and more customers get to know and love your gig. I get a lot of return customers, because once they know you can reliably deliver a great gig (which is a great deal for them) and that you are pleasant and accommodating to deal with, they will come back again and again.

Many good Fiverr sellers offer free extras for their customers. For example, if they are creating links for you, they might say "I gave you an extra five links as a free bonus". People love free extras, and if it guarantees that your customer will leave you with a warm, fuzzy feeling and give you a great review it can really be worth giving bonuses or extras. This also creates customer loyalty - why would they go to someone else next time if you did a great job and gave them extra? This is a great strategy to use.

By now, you should be realizing what a gold mine Fiverr really is - you really can make money online if you know where to look. Many people are making $500 to $1000 a month on Fiverr, and you can be one of them. I'm hoping for even better for you - with these techniques you should be able to make it to top seller status. I could definitely have gone that route - I was on my way until I discovered an even better way to make money online. I still offer Fiverr gigs, but it is no longer my main focus - I started my own publishing company with seed money that I made on Fiverr over the summer and that's what I'm currently building. Read on if you'd like to learn how to make money with Kindle Publishing.

There are some other sites like Fiverr - some of them are uphype.com, gighour.com, justafive.com, and gigme5.com. There are actually about 20 different ones, but some of them are in other countries and pay in euros, etc. I've investigated several of them, and based on their sites and common knowledge, Fiverr is the most profitable by far. However, I expect these other ones to improve with time, gain page rank, and become more popular. So, once you get some great gigs that sell you could branch out to other sites for even more sales potential. Just something to keep in mind for the future.

Fiverr has lots of success stories where people were able to start businesses there and make a lot of money doing it. If you'd like to have an online presence where you can offer services to customers, Fiverr.com may be just what you're looking for. Plus, this is an opportunity you can start right now…today.

Here's a link to www.Fiverr.com .

Conclusion

We've made it to the end of our lesson on how to make money online at Fiverr. Let's recap a little to refresh what you've learned. First of all, we covered Fiverr - what it is, how it works, how much money people are making, and what they do with the extra income they make from the site. I explained about gigs, gig extras, seller levels, and customer reviews. I also included information on how to find those popular gigs with high sales volume - the kinds of gigs you want to offer to make a lot of money on Fiverr. We've learned how to look at a gig on Fiverr and determine how well it sells based on the number of reviews, the dates on the reviews, and when the gig was created. We also talked about the order queue - how many orders are in queue and how that can tell us how well a gig is selling.

We also covered the importance of treating your Fiverr business like a real business. It is taxable income, of course, so you need to report it on your taxes. You need to set aside a time each day to work on your gigs, and spend some time daily on the site so you can check for messages and orders. Your Fiverr rating is essential to high sales, so maintain it at 100% or as close to it as possible. We talked about ways to keep your rating high. Keep customers coming back by over delivering, offering exceptional customer service in a world that has forgotten what that is, and regularly communicating with the customer while working on their order. Wouldn't you like to know the status of your order? Great reviews are also a must, so make sure that when you deliver a gig that you put in a message that if there are any problems, the buyer should contact you and you will make revisions or fix the problems.

Get lots of successful orders done so that you can reach Level 2 status as quickly as possible. With Gigextras, we can do fewer gigs and make more money. Level 2 status also helps us to come up higher in the search results when someone searches for a particular gig on the site.

We've also discussed SEO and how to write gig titles and descriptions that will allow you to come up higher in the search engine on the Fiverr site. Remember to use your keywords close to the beginning of your gig title and also in the first sentence in your gig description. Also, pick the proper tags for your gig so that people can find it.

This is a learning process - much like life itself. As you get more experience on the site, you will become more and more successful. The tips you've learned here will save you a lot of time and allow you to start making money sooner. Now, let's talk about Kindle Direct Publishing!

Introduction to KDP

"Holy Shit!"

That's what my husband said when I showed him my first Amazon Kindle Publishing royalties statement. The next thing he said was, "I should write a book."

I have to say I was pretty surprised myself. I had expected to make maybe $50 a month to start, and then add some more books to perhaps get my Kindle ebook revenues up to a few hundred dollars a month ($200 to $300 perhaps). Not anything life-changing, but I like doing little projects and experiments in online business, and publishing a Kindle ebook sounded fun to me. I especially like residual income from writing, so Kindle was an interesting venture to me. Boy, was I surprised when the revenues were quickly (within a few months) ten times what I had originally expected, based on my experience with other online money-making methods. Apparently, I had vastly underestimated the power that is Amazon.

Anyway, I can't believe I wasted so much time writing hundreds of Ehow articles (only to have them pull out the rug from under all the writers and buy them out). With a little over a hundred Ehow articles, my royalties were about $300 a month (not bad and I was still growing it). I got bought out (pretty much they said we're taking all your articles off the site - we're willing to buy you out (all my articles) for a few thousand dollars or you get nothing). I took the money and moved on.

I never made any money on Bukisa (cents), did some writing for Mahalo (more peanuts), and finally found my way to something successful - Fiverr.com. I became pretty successful on Fiverr, making over $1000 a month in my spare time. I did "gigs" for customers - originally for $4 each but the money you can charge for services and packages has gone up radically since then. My average sale was around $30. Then, I moved on from there when I discovered online publishing. I guess I really am an indie publisher at heart...

Discovering Kindle Publishing

By getting very familiar with "everything Fiverr" I came across Kindle Publishing quite by accident. I noticed a lot of gigs had to do with Kindle ebooks - a lot of people seemed to be doing it. People were offering to market other people's Kindle ebooks, edit them, format them to be uploaded to Kindle, make covers for Kindle books, write Kindle ebook descriptions for authors, and so on. Hmmmm, I thought. Maybe there's something to this Kindle publishing thing. And, even better, here's all these people who are willing to format the book, design a cover for it, market it, etc. for a very low cost (all the things I don't know how to do - because I knew nothing about Kindle publishing then). I decided the time was right for a Kindle ebook experiment...

I knew I had a lot of information about making money online - I'd tried pretty much everything from starting a blog (not an easy way to make money) to online writing, to micro-enterprise sites such as Fiverr and Elance. I wrote a book about my experiences and ways to make money, my first one. I then hired a woman on Fiverr to make the cover for it - she even came up with the illustration on the cover for me as part of the

$5 fee! I had her do the cover for the Fiverr book I wrote at the time also, so that they would be similar. She was very helpful, answering all my questions - and I had a lot of them at the time.

I hired another woman to format the book for Kindle for me. She did a great job, and again answered all my questions (she was super helpful). She told me, "Hon, you need a cover first". I didn't know that, but I was learning all about Kindle publishing. I wrote the book, had the cover made, and had the book formatted in only a few weeks. To my amazement, I was easily able to sign up for Kindle Direct Publishing via the Amazon site (I already had an Amazon account), and I uploaded the book by myself with no problems. I was really surprised at just how easy it was! Imagine my shock when I checked my Kindle publishing statistics a few hours later and found I'd sold 3 books (making $6.24). Automated, residual income from publishing - my new love. That was way back in September 2012. A lot has changed since then!

I'm going to back up here a little bit and define residual income as I realize not everyone is familiar with the term. Residual income is money that comes in long after you've done the work. I wrote an online course when my daughter was born. She's in college now – almost done actually. I've been collecting substantial royalties (over two thousand dollars a month) every month since 1997 from the work I did (in 1997) writing that course. That's residual income - you do the work once and collect money indefinitely. Turning back to Kindle, I now wake up each morning and look to see how much money I made on Kindle sales while I slept. It's nice being paid to sleep. My younger daughter recently looked at my daily spreadsheet of Kindle sales and said, "Mom - that's like winning at Bingo every single day!" So, I guess everyone looks at it differently…

Another great thing that you need to realize about residual income is that sales occur 365 days a year, and 24 hours a day. So, each month, instead of working 8 hours a day, 5 days a week (40 hours a week), for a total of 160 hours per month, your book(s) is on sale 24 hours a day, 7 days a week (168 hours times 4 weeks is 672 hours). Therefore, even if you make less per hour than at a "real job", your sales are taking place 4.2 times as many hours as you would spend at a normal job. That 4.2 times is a powerful multiplier. When I'm sick, sales still roll in. When I'm clothes shopping on Saturdays with my daughters, sales are rolling in. I can do whatever I want - and sales are rolling in. It's unbelievable. I think of my books as little workers that work for free - on holidays, through the night, every day of the year, 24/7. They never complain, either.

Believe me - if you want to make your husband or wife really happy, find a way to automatically generate money to pay your mortgage every month!

My 'Top Secret' Secrets?

Now you're probably wondering why I'm writing a book telling everyone about Kindle Publishing. Isn't that just creating competition for myself? Well, not really. First of all, I wouldn't be the first or only person to write on this subject - lots of information is already out there. Some books are great, some are just a bunch of hype and baloney. Most of them are written by men, and I know that women look at things differently than men do, and also learn in different ways. That's why I'm writing a book - to tell you my personal story and how you could do it, too - regardless if you're a man or a woman.

Secondly, for every person who reads about a real way to make income, only a very small percentage (much less than 5%) actually go the next step and do what's needed to be successful. Many readers might want to read my story, but won't be serious enough to do this themselves. I love reading about other people's lives and businesses, real estate ventures, etc. but I don't go into all of those businesses. My husband always asks why I watch shows like Wife Swap - it's because I like to see how other people live (and yes, I do know these aren't as real as the producers might want you to think). Still, you can get some good ideas that you could incorporate into your life - or not. I just find it interesting to see how others design their lives. Perhaps I should've been a sociologist. Anyway, I like reading books written by many different people, and I know other people do as well.

Thirdly, Kindle ebooks are different than other products. They don't compete with each other as much as some products do. For example, if I was going to spend $100 on an expensive electric toothbrush, I would look at all the alternatives and then choose one. However, if I wanted to learn about starting a business on Fiverr, I would buy all of the most successful Fiverr ebooks in the Kindle store. Why? Because I would learn a little from each one, and in each, get a different person's perspective and many different techniques and ideas. Many Kindle ebooks are $2.99 or so, meaning you can buy 8 different ones and still have only invested $24. That's some pretty cheap education! I've been an indie Kindle publisher for five years now, and I've read many books on the subject of Kindle publishing for my own education. When it really came down to it, though, I did things my own way. I guess that's just me.

There's another reason that I'm willing to share my secrets about publishing. Amazon is very good at "killing" spam ebooks. If you write a quick book that isn't helpful (in the case of nonfiction) or entertaining (in the case of fiction books), you won't sell many books. Spammers may be able to get some friends to put up great reviews about their book, but once real customers start buying the book they will rip it apart in the reviews. Then, no one else buys it. Its rank falls into the millions – yes, that's right - millions. Then they give up. Now, on the other hand, if an author creates a quality product that customers want, I believe they should be entitled to sell it on Amazon along with other authors' books. In our market-based economy, the people decide with their buying dollars which products thrive and which will die.

I finally decided to write a Kindle Publishing ebook when

I had initially decided not to. Why? There is just so much incorrect information out there! I've read many Kindle Publishing ebooks that say "you can't simply pay someone $5 or $10 to create a cover for you and be successful." I laugh out loud every time I read that - because that's what I've done many, many times. Granted, great covers are necessary, but you don't have to pay $200 for one. There are many talented people out there looking for work right now.

I also read a lot about how you have to have a blog or create a list of emails (by collecting people's emails on your blog or site) that you can send out to people whenever you launch a new book. I don't have a blog regarding my books. Perhaps in the future I will, but there's a good chance I won't. I've done great with Amazon kindle sales without a blog, without a following of readers like some big authors have, without using Facebook, Twitter, or anything else. There's simply a lot of people on Amazon, and with proper SEO (search engine optimization) they will find your book. I don't spend time creating backlinks to make my product page more popular (although I do know how to do this from working at Ehow and Hubpages). Additionally, I hate the idea of collecting people's emails on a site only to inundate them with email after email trying to get them to buy something – even ebooks. That I would never do - it's just not me.

I choose to spend my time writing - my true love - and let Amazon sell my ebooks. A major factor in making money online is a website's authority with Google's search engine. So, if you are creating your own blog or website, you start out with a 'no authority site' (unless you buy an established site from someone else). You spend years trying to build up your site's authority so it will show up high in Google search results. With Amazon, they already have tremendous authority with Google - they are one of the highest. So, just having your product on Amazon means it'll sell more than it would on your "no-name" site or blog. That's why I gave up my own websites. I had created some Wordpress sites and put articles on them to make Google Adsense income a few years ago - quite unsuccessfully. It's definitely not easy. That's why people who write articles for Adsense income are smart if they do so on a site that already has authority and not on their own site (sharing the Adsense revenue with the site owner). In any event, my point is you can't believe everything people say about Kindle Publishing.

Covers - So Very Important

Let's get back to covers. I've already told you that you can find a cover designer (actually many of them) on Fiverr.com. Look for a cover designer that has a lot of orders in queue. That means many people have hired them and they are good - busily working on many orders. Read the reviews - they should have a lot of recent (written within the last day or two) reviews and they should be excellent. This is also reflected in their rating (gig rating and user rating). All of this information is on their gig page (that pops up when you click on their gig in the listing). Look at how long they will take to deliver your gig (est. delivery). On many of the gigs, you can now see samples of their work like covers they've done recently.

I always carefully research a gig and a seller before buying any gig. Being from the US, I usually look for someone in the US, Canada, or the UK - just because there are a lot of scams that originate in foreign countries. They also speak fluent English - always a bonus for an English-speaking author writing a book in English. If there's a lot of mistakes in their gig description, that's not a good sign. Move on to the next one.

The cover artist I normally use always has a lot of orders in queue, but I get around that by paying the extra $5 or $10 to have my order completed in 24 hours. She always meets the deadline!

As I mentioned, my first few covers were illustrations created by my cover artist. I did this so the books would look like they belong together and aren't totally different in theme and appearance. However, many of my Kindle ebooks have covers that feature photographs. You can use royalty-free photos and clipart. Royalty-free does not mean the photos are free - only that you can purchase a license to use them. Always read the licensing agreement prior to purchasing. You can usually use the photo on a cover many times (read the agreement). However, others can also do so - you aren't the exclusive user of the picture. Many licensing agreements restrict the use of pictures for adult content, etc. Read the site's agreement all the way through. There is sometimes a regular license and an extended one for additional uses. The extended licenses cost more than a regular one. Again, the different types of licenses are outlined on the sites. Sometimes the extended licenses offer more liability coverage than a regular one does. Read the agreement...did I say that enough times?

Some sites you can check out to buy a photograph license from istockphoto (you can join or buy photo licenses individually with credits that you purchase on the site- photos range from less than $10 and up or buy a subscription if you plan on downloading a number of photos), and freedigitalphotos.net. You can find many similar photo sites by searching for royalty free photos or pictures on Google.

To be honest, I don't have any subscriptions for photograph sites just yet. I have been buying my photos individually on the sites listed. I pay about $20 to $25 for each cover photo license I buy. This is mainly because I was doing my Kindle publishing experiment and didn't want to break the bank doing it. A fundamental rule in business is that you start small and lean, then grow from there. You can find some very nice photos for $8-10 also, depending on the site. In the future, I may get a subscription. If I write two books a month, that would be $40 to $50 dollars a month on cover photos ($480 to $600 per year) so a subscription may be the right way for me to go in the future.

When picking a photo for a cover, I decide whether I want

a vector type illustration or a real photograph. For some subjects, I use real photos on the cover and for others I use a vector drawing. I do whichever I feel matches the subject matter best. Sometimes I have to actually go to a photo site and look at what's available in order to make the decision - drawing or photo. Also, if I find something perfect, I'll use it whether it's a drawing or photo. Anything I like, I save that photo's page on my Favorites on my laptop. That way, I can choose from between my possibilities afterward.

As far as photos and illustrations go, I look for bright colors. I try to imagine how the title will look with the picture. I think simpler is better - not a cluttered photo. I look for a picture or vector that is attention-getting. It's going to have to compete with many other pictures, even as a little thumbnail. So, I like bright, simple, and attention-drawing.

Look for the most professional-looking picture you can find. It shouldn't look like one from a family album. The picture also needs to go along with the topic of your book - have the same feeling. If it doesn't feel right, forget it and move on. I usually save about ten pictures or so (depending on the book topic - sometimes there are very slim pickings and I can only find two or three possible choices) in the Favorites on my computer. Then, I narrow them down from that. Sometimes I get family members' opinions on what photo they find most interesting. Ultimately, I make the decision.

Usually I have an idea of what I want on the cover. I type that into the search engine on the photo site to pull up pages and pages of photos. Depending on the site, you can usually narrow the search to just illustrations under $20, for example. I usually flip through pages of photos and/or illustrations while watching television at night - because it takes a while to find the perfect cover image. I actually enjoy this part of the publishing process!

I'm especially careful about model releases. Any picture

that shows a person (especially a child) requires a model release to use their image. So, for a picture of just feet in the sand you may not need a model release, but a woman's face would definitely require one. A model release may be difficult to get for a photo you find on a stock photo site - for obvious reasons. So, I avoid using any picture that may need a model release - no people's faces. Some websites even claim model releases are needed for just pictures of parts of the body with no head if they are distinctive. It's a pretty complicated matter. If I need to depict a person, I use an illustration instead of a photo. If I need an image of a rose, I would use a real photograph. Again, read all the information on the photo site to avoid future litigation problems.

After you find your perfect picture or illustration, you are ready to have your cover made. My best advice is don't do it yourself - unless you're a professional graphic artist. It just won't look professional - no matter how hard you try. Just spend some time on Amazon, and you can tell who did their own crappy cover. Hire a graphic artist to do the cover, whether it's on Fiverr or Elance or wherever. Make sure you are as explicit as possible in telling the person what you want - providing them with links to covers you like is usually helpful to give them an idea. Remember - a picture is worth a thousand words.

You should have the cover done first, as you will need to give the cover file plus your ebook document (likely as an MS Word file) to whomever is going to format your ebook for Kindle. If they're a good formatter, they will include the cover inside of the document (at the beginning). Also, ask the person formattting your Kindle if they will do a clickable TOC (table of contents) so that readers can click on links in the table of contents and be brought to that place in the ebook. Formatting with pictures/recipes/children's picture books is more complex, so you will have to pay more to have those kinds of ebooks formatted.

The Kindle Publishing Process

Next, you just upload the file you got from the formatter and the cover you got from the graphic artist to the Kindle Store at Amazon. This is pretty simple. Once you're at your KDP (Kindle Direct Publishing) Bookshelf (after signing into your account), you simply click 'add a new title' and you can start putting in your new book. It will ask you things like Book Name, Publisher (optional), Description (where you put the description of the book that will show on your book's page on Amazon), Book contributors (you can just put author if you want), language, and publishing date (optional). It will ask you if you want to enroll the book in KDP Select on this first page, so I'll go over that now.

KDP Select enrollment means you are allowing people who are KDP Select Members (they pay a special fee to Amazon) to rent your book. This used to be awesome back when publishers were paid for each rental based on what the monthly revenue pot had in it. In my experience, I got very close to what I would make on a book sale (a regular royalty for a $2.99 sale is $2.08), so I enrolled all my books in it. Royalties can add up to thousands of dollars a month. My highest revenue month from KDP was $4000.

Now, unfortunately, we indie publishers who join KDP Select and allow Amazon to rent our books make much less. They switched to KENP, which basically means we are now paid a little less than $.005 per page read (this per page rate goes up and down on a monthly basis but this is an approximation), based on what the monthly revenue pot has in it. Also, some countries have lower pay than that, depending on the country. Anyway, now we're paid only for what pages borrowers actually read, and the payment is a lot less than it was before. Before, it didn't matter how long your books were – you were paid for the book rental. Now, if you write a 150 page book, you'll get $.75 instead of the approximate $1.40 per book we used to make (no matter how long the book was) if the person reads the whole book. So, you can still obviously make money doing this, but it's not nearly the gold mine it used to be. And, today there is a lot more competition on Amazon than there was in say 2012. For Select, you have to enroll books for a 90 day term, and books will automatically be re-enrolled unless you go in and un-enroll them. Un-enrolling it will not affect the current term, however. You'll have to wait for the three-month term to be up to be officially un-enrolled and be able to publish elsewhere.

The main thing you need to know about KDP Select is that you can not have your ebook sold anywhere else if you are enrolled in KDP Select. You are exclusively giving Amazon the right to sell your ebook. While enrolled, you can't sell it on Smashwords, your own site - anywhere else. Just Amazon. So, authors have to decide whether it's worth it to give up all other sales avenues (Smashwords, Barnes and Noble Nook, Apple, etc.) in order to be enrolled. For me, it's worth it. Anyway, make sure you read the terms of the KDP Select so you know what you're getting into before enrolling.

After that, they will ask you to verify your publishing rights (if you wrote it yourself or someone else wrote it and you own the rights to it, you click on 'Not a public domain work, and I hold the necessary publishing rights'). You then add categories, keywords (7 of them), and upload the cover and the book file itself. We'll discuss more on categories and keywords later - right now I'm just going over the publishing process for you. You can then preview the ebook if you like (I don't - I publish it and then make changes later if necessary). I've read that the previews don't work well, so I've never used them. I don't know this personally to be true, though. Perhaps that's changed by now.

Hit Save and Continue. Next, you verify the publishing territories. I hit "worldwide rights" because I always have those - I write my own books so I have all the rights. Then, you choose your royalty. I do a $2.99 price to start with usually, so that I get the 70% royalty (you click on 70%). If you choose a lower price, you will get the 35% royalty. Then, for each country listed I click on 'set price automatically based on US price. If you like, you can try starting out at 99 cents and a 35% royalty - its up to you, the publisher.

Now, you can either click on 'Allow lending for this book' or not. I always allow lending, because I think it's a nice thing to do. You can choose not to click on it if you like. There's a thorough description of what lending entails - basically it allows people who purchase your book to lend it to friends and family. The lender can't read the book while it's lent out and each book can only be lent out once for 14 days. There are some other restrictions that are outlined right there on the page if you want more information.

Next, you click on the final statement that says by clicking Save and Publish, you're confirming that you hold the necessary rights to publish the ebook, will abide by their terms (which you should read - click on them). Finally, you click Save and Publish. Done! Yay!

You can then go to your Bookshelf, which will show your book is in the publishing process. It usually takes about 12 hours for it to go live in my experience. I usually publish at night (8 or 9 o'clock) and its active in the morning or shortly thereafter. Once your book shows as being published on your Bookshelf, you can type the title and author into the search engine on the Amazon.com and look at your book's Amazon page - very cool, no matter how many times you publish. Time to rinse and repeat...

Picking Profitable Topics for Your Ebooks

Now that we've covered publishing on Amazon, let's back way up. The topic you choose for your Kindle ebook is absolutely crucial to your success. I'll say it again for emphasis-the topic you choose for your Kindle ebook is absolutely crucial to your success. If people aren't buying books on How to Start a Babysitting Service, then don't write an ebook about how to start a babysitting service. You won't make any money. You can't create demand for a certain topic, but the good news is that you do have the flexibility to choose the topic of your ebook before you write it.

You're in charge - just research before you write - not afterwards. Your time is valuable. If you've spent weeks writing an ebook that there is no or little demand for, you've essentially wasted those weeks. The opportunity cost in business is what you could have done if you hadn't done something. So, time wasted writing a book that won't sell is time you could've spent writing a book that would generate $100 or more a month.

We're only looking at other ebooks on Amazon to get ideas about topics. I am certainly not advising you to make copycat books, like many spammers do. This is pretty apparent to customers (they copy your book title or as much as possible), the spammers get bad reviews, and don't do well in the long run. Once you find a good subject, look at what's currently available. How could you do something similar, but with a different spin on it? You don't want to be the same as other books - how would you stand out? If you have experience related to the topic (that would be best and easiest to write), then you definitely have your own story to tell about your own personal journey with this subject.

This ebook I'm writing is a perfect example - there's lots of books on Kindle Publishing: Formatting for Kindle, the Kindle Bible, How to Come up with Non-Fiction Kindle Ideas, How to Write an Ebook in a Week and so on (these aren't all actual titles, but there are books very similar to these). When it comes down to it, no one has my experience with Kindle Publishing. No one picks a cover, writes a book, and publishes their Kindle ebooks the same way as I do. My books are more successful than many other authors, who make next to no sales at all. I know this because I read blogs about people who have made only a couple hundred dollars in six months on their ebooks (Kindle sales included). I make thousands a month.

I've been very successful, I have five years of experience publishing on Kindle, and I make the money that comes from that growth in my indie publishing experience. In fact, the Kindle Publishing ebook I write will be like no one else's. That's the competitive edge I have. I'm not trying to boast here - just to let you know what is sometimes possible.

Think of the ebook you want to write, whether it's about a hobby you have or a skill you picked up from your job. I always suggest people start with something they know a great deal about - it makes writing so much easier! Once you come up with a list of topics, check Amazon to see if books like your topic are selling. How do we know if they're selling? We check the book's rank on Amazon (after the book description – you usually have to scroll down to see this – it's down by where the publisher is listed). We're going to write the hot topics first, and maybe someday, if we have totally run out of better ideas, we'll write the not-so-hot topics. Maybe, maybe not…

Hiring Someone Else to Write Your Book - and Why I Don't Do It

Many Kindle publishing books I've read advise you to outsource the writing of your books to someone else that you find on a website (perhaps Upwork or Fiverr for example). I thought about this, being a business person and knowing I could publish many more books in less time if I were to hire writers. They would write my books for a flat fee, giving me all the rights to the books. I decided not to do this for several reasons, and I will outline them here for you. You can make this decision for yourself, of course.

First of all, I would have to find someone who writes like I do, or I would just end up rewriting the book. Secondly, I would have to carefully run each book through software to make sure none of it was plagiarized or lifted from somewhere else before posting it on Amazon. I would have to work on the writer's timeline - and many would require a lengthy amount of time (a month, 2 months) to write a book that I could probably get done much faster. I would also be adding another person into the mix, and dealing with them would take up some of my time. To hire a good writer, I would have to pay them a reasonably large amount of money ($500 to $1000) - whereas I write for myself for free. In the end, I just decided it wasn't worth it for me. I don't want to mass-produce junk - I want to share my experiences with the world in order to help other people do what I do. I guess world-domination will just have to wait...

SEO is Important!

Many Kindle experts swear by using a keyword tool to check to see if a topic is being searched by a lot of people per month. I use keyword tools, but I believe looking on Amazon is a much more reliable method of anticipating customer demand for a specific topic. I know a lot of people are looking for information on how to do various things, but sometimes they aren't willing to buy a Kindle book on Amazon to do it. They are probably using free information on websites instead. You can always use an external Keyword Tool to find additional keywords afterwards, but for topics I use Amazon itself. This is where SEO (search engine optimization) comes into play as far as Kindle ebooks go. Once you find well-searched keywords on the Keyword Tool (like Merchantwords for example), you can incorporate them into your book's title, its description, and the keywords you put on the book when you upload it to Kindle.

If you don't know much about SEO, learn about it. There are many tutorials and articles related to learning SEO that are available for free on the internet. Do a Google search - I learned everything I know about SEO for free on the net. Even just learning the basics will help you enormously. It's a bit complex as you get in deeper and deeper (I've studied it for years), but just the basics will be invaluable to you as a Kindle publisher. This is what most authors need to know that they don't - and their books reside in the Amazon cellar. SEO is the secret…great keywords used properly will bring Amazon's traffic to your door (product page). This is assuming there is significant demand for your topic - so check that first!

We're also going to use the Amazon search engine to see what's popular on the site. Ever notice when you're searching for something on Amazon, it starts to offer you suggestions to complete your search? You type in 'vampire' and it offers you a choice of 'vampire diaries', 'vampire weekend', 'vampire knight', and 'Buffy the vampire slayer,' to name a few. Guess what? These are the most popular searches related to the word 'vampire' on Amazon. They are so helpful!

By using Amazon's search engine and looking at the top books related to your prospective topic (and their rank), you should be able to make a relatively quick decision about whether such a book would be worthwhile for you. Remember your list of prospective topics? Start crossing off those that look like duds that won't make money. Narrow your list down until you find a good topic. Maybe none of your prospective topics will be viable. In that case, start searching Amazon for good topics, checking the related books and their ranks.

Write a Good Book

Take the time to write a really good book, if not a great book. What are you offering people? Are you telling them something they don't already know? Is it interesting? Are you giving specifics? My biggest pet peeve is books that offer only generalizations and popular sayings and/or advice. If I'm not getting anything new out of it, what's the point? If you're aren't going to give me real instruction, why am I reading? Time is money. You could be writing a profitable book instead of reading some guru's book full of puns and general information.

Is your book well-written? Has it been edited? Every book has a typo or two, but some ebooks on Amazon are so badly written or have so many typos that you literally can't read them.

Some are written by people who don't even speak English! Don't be one of those books. Customers will kill you in the reviews, and you'll end up with all the others in Amazon's basement. That's not the place to be - no money, very sad.

Once you have your topic and keywords to use in your book, write it. Hopefully, you'll have enough knowledge on the subject to just write it. If not, do some research until you do have the knowledge you need to write a good book on that topic. Whatever you do, do not plagiarize. Amazon's bots will pick it up very quickly if the material is elsewhere on the internet, and you could have your account closed. Yikes! Don't even dare - write your own book. (I know you wouldn't do it, but I feel the need to warn you anyways as the penalty is so disastrous to our plan to make you successful at this).

No Fluff!

Many Kindle publishing gurus suggest you add lots of filler to make your book longer. This is because customers sometimes look at the number of pages in your ebook when deciding whether it's worth purchasing. And now, with KENP – remember? Longer books make more money. Still, I don't like added fluff. I don't like people wasting my time - I just said that three paragraphs ago. You can fill up an ebook with tons of resources online and links to this or that - and I know I won't ever look at them. If you have a few helpful resources, by all means include them. Otherwise, forget it. Just write the book, including what's necessary but with no extra fluff. Customers are really smart - they know fluff when they see it.

I also advise against incorporating lots of extra pages at the beginning of your ebook. Normally, you have the cover image, a title page, a copyright page, a table of contents, and then the ebook starts (like this ebook). I feel this is best. When people hit the 'Look Inside' feature on Amazon to see the beginning of your book, they want to know if they'll like the book. Let them read some of the book, and not just a bunch of crazy pre-book pages. Hook them - show them you're a good writer, and you know what you're talking about. Prospective customers want to know that your book isn't spam (or just a hook to get you to buy something else) before they buy it. Let them want to read more of your book, and to learn more from you. A bunch of extra pages won't tell them anything about you as a writer or how interesting your book is. It's just annoying.

The reason many "experts" say to do the "extra superfluous pages in the beginning" is because they don't want to show customers what's in the content of their book until the customer buys it. I say, 'Big deal if someone gets to read the first few pages for free". Why? Because they can always get a refund if they buy the book, read the whole thing, and don't like it anyways. A sale isn't iron-clad. This is business - you'll have sales, and you'll have refunds (mine are only about 1% so nothing I even consider). Some people just read the books and request a refund - all the time - no matter how good the book is. They just wanted to read it, and don't want to keep it. I say include enough great information in your ebooks to make people want to keep them as a future resource. Give them information they will want to reference in the future. The point here: Use your book introduction as a sales tool to help the customer make the decision that this is a book they want to read. That's the whole idea of a "Look Inside" preview. Amazon knows that - that's why they have the "Look Inside" preview in the first place. They want to sell books - just like we do.

In my reviews, customers often write statements like "she gets right to the point" and "the author is very straightforward" and "she just tells you what you need to know". These statements, to me, show that most people, like myself, want to know the information they bought the book for and then get to work on it. They don't want to waste their time, and rightly so!

Pricing Strategies for Maximum Profit

I like a $2.99 price for my ebooks. My books are not terribly long, so I wouldn't charge more for them. If we go lower than $2.99 given Amazon's current royalty structure, we will get a 35% royalty instead of a 70% royalty. So, at $.99 we make about $.35 per book. At $1.99, we make about $.70. At $2.99, we make $2.08. I like a little over $2 as a royalty a lot better than 35 cents (it's almost 6 times as much). We would have to sell six times as many books at $.99 to make the commission we will make on one book at $2.99. I've played around with my spreadsheet, changing prices to see the effects. I simply am more profitable at the $2.99 price.

Do I ever charge $.99 cents for one of my books? Absolutely! If my Amazon rank for a book is really tanking, I change the keywords, rewrite the book description, possibly change the cover, and lower the price to $.99 until the rank gets back up to where I want it. During a promotion, I give away the books for free. I gave away 10,201 copies of my most popular book within three days in April 2013. I didn't even promote it on free ebook websites, and it still had that many downloads. The rank for that book soared all the way up to the top 10 list for free books on Amazon. After the promotion, the sales skyrocketed. I'll discuss more about promotions later in this book.

As far as pricing goes, if a book is non-fiction and should have a good deal of natural demand (because we carefully researched the topic), then I'll start it out at $2.99. If I am publishing a fiction book that will have a lot of competition, I will start it out at $.99 until its ranking gets up to an acceptable level. I consider an acceptable level 30,000 or lower for these types of books. The lower the rank, the higher the sales per day.

If, someday, I write a much longer book, I may price it higher than $2.99. I have a terrific spreadsheet that I keep daily to tell me how price changes, promotions, keyword changes, etc. affect daily sales. I would price the book higher and see how daily sales go. Then, I might drop it for two weeks to see what affect that has on sales. I figure out at what price I make the most money, and keep it there. If sales start to tank, I lower the price. Anyone familiar with economics knows that there is an inverse relationship between price and demand. Those two things are opposites. As price goes up, demand for a product goes down. As price goes down, demand for a product goes up. We have to figure out if a lower price increases demand (in terms of daily sales) enough to make it worthwhile. At what price do we make the most money? That's the name of the game…

I don't care what price I sell my ebooks at. I would sell them at a penny a piece if demand at that price was high enough to make me the largest amount of money. We care about our total revenue and profit, not the actual price we charge for the ebook. Some authors won't drop the price of their books because they feel their books are "worth more than that". Let's be real - this is business. Smart business people care about the amount of money they make and not the price of each book. My philosophy as a writer and publisher is that I am selling a book, not my soul. I won't let foolish pride stand in the way of making a reasonable amount of money on my books.

My Awesome Spreadsheet

Since the first day I published on Amazon, I have kept a Microsoft Works spreadsheet of daily sales. Amazon only gives you a total figure of sales (in units) for each book for the month so far. They will only let you look back 90 days on their system. The only way to track daily sales, sales promotions, price changes, and so on is to keep a spreadsheet of your own. Mine says the month at the top, with my books (the titles) listed down vertically under the month. For each column, I write in a date (horizontally across the spreadsheet (in numbers)), with each box in the spreadsheet representing a day of the month. Each day, I fill in how many of each book have been sold for the month up to that point. I check it at 9am and 11pm. That's when I update the numbers. Sometimes I also do it mid-day, but not always. It just depends on how busy I am that particular day - and whether I'm home or not.

In addition to daily sales, I also chart pages read for KENP each day. That way, I know how much I've made daily (and monthly) for both sales and borrows.

I have the total books sold for the month at the bottom of each column, along with the total number of books sold that day. I also include the total sales figure for the day ($81.56 for example) at the top of each day's column (under the date). I mark on each day if I have a price change and what amount, if I start a certain promo, end a promo, and any other information I want to mark on a day. I do this underneath the daily total at the bottom of the column. That way, when I look back afterwards, I can see that my sales for Book #1 went from 8 a day to 13 a day when I changed the price from $2.99 to $1.99.

Strategically, you won't be able to handle your publishing account without a spreadsheet similar to this. Amazon just doesn't give us as indie publishers the stats we need to make good decisions about our books. I also have all of the daily totals added up at the end of the month (by having the spreadsheet sum all the daily totals across). I can see how many total books have been sold by having a total underneath the last day of the month. You don't need to set it up just like mine - just make a spreadsheet that will give you all this information and that makes sense to you.

Here's a list of what you want to keep track of on the spreadsheet you make (or have someone who knows how to set up a spreadsheet help you). You want daily sales (in terms of units) for each individual book. You want total KENP per day. You want a total sales figure (in dollars) for each day. You want a total number of books sold per day. Then, you want the daily sales to total automatically to give you a running total of sales (in dollars) for the month. Also, have a running total of the number of books sold for the month (by adding up the daily book sales in units).

Remember that KDP Select can automatically put your books in for the next three month period when one three month period ends. You can't get out of it during the three month period - you have to wait for that three month period to expire. So, read up on it and make sure you understand all about it before signing up for the KDP Select rental program.

Top Places to Advertise Kindle Free Book Days

I make it a point to stay on top of my books - I check their rank on Amazon (on the product page) and I also check the rank of the other top books that are similar to see how they are doing. Sometimes I change the price of the book to see the effect on sales. Because KDP Select books get 5 days every 3 months to have a free promo, you can sometimes schedule a promotion if your sales are dropping along with your ranking. The more free downloads, the more it will help sales of that book after it is taken off the free promo. Lots of free downloads increases your rank, and it maintains that rank for a bit after the book is taken off promo. So, the book gets more exposure to customers on Amazon, and thus more sales. If you have few downloads (a few hundred to a few thousand), this benefit won't occur (or occur to a much smaller extent). That's why many authors submit their book to "free kindle book sites" and blogs - so more people will know when their book will be on free promo and will download it.

Here's a list of twelve places you can submit information about your free promo days.

http://www.freeebooksdaily.com

http://thedigitalinkspot.blogspot.com

http://blog.booksontheknob.org

http://www.bookgorilla.com

http://bargainebookhunter.com

http://incredibleindieebooks.blogspot.com

http://www.freebookdude.com

http://www.thatbookplace.com

http://www.frugal-freebies.com

http://thefrugalereader.com

http://www.daily-free-ebooks.com

http://www.fkbooksandtips.com

You'll need to read the material on each site for any restrictions (a few may charge a fee, some will only let you put on a book with 10 or more good reviews, some will only let you advertise a book that will be free within the next 24 hours, others require a week's notice between you contacting them and your book's free days). I'll get more into my opinion of this strategy later on in the book (under Marketing).

Your Amazon Product Page - and How to Make It Great

Now let's talk about your product page.

Your product page on Amazon will include a lot of different elements - an image of your book cover, the title of your book, author name, publisher name (optional), date published, rank, price, number of reviews, reviews themselves, your product description, language, your ASIN number, file size of your book, what books people also bought when they purchased your book, about the author section (if you make one), and many, many other items. The best way to see everything on a page is to go to Amazon and check out a Kindle ebook product page.

Because I just mentioned the About the Author section, I will make some comments on that. Make an About the Author section. You access this via your KDP Bookshelf. At the top of it is your Publishing Account. Click on that, sign in, and once you're in your publishing account you can create an About the Author section that will show up on your book's page on Amazon.

I will also mention pen names here. I use pen names for my books because I have a varied set of expertise, and it would be confusing to have me writing books on many subjects that have nothing to do with each other. That would confuse my customers. I also like to maintain my privacy and that of my family as I discuss them in some of my books. Amazon allows authors to use pen names, and if you don't want the credit for writing your books, feel free to use them. You also set them up via your Publishing Account. You can even have different pen names and descriptions on different books. Amazon has you set up an author profile and then has you choose the books that are yours under that pen name. You can then set up another author profile, and choose the books that are associated with that pen name. I believe there is currently a limit of three pen names you can use (3 author profiles) on Amazon.

I'm a real person, everything I talk about is what I've done (does it sound like I know what I'm talking about?), and what I include in my About the Author is true information about my life. The pictures I include are of my pets, flowers in my yard, and photos I've taken on vacation. The only difference is the name, which I like to protect in this age of identity theft, internet information, etc. I had my credit card hacked via the internet before, and the person ran up plane tickets on Jet Blue and all kinds of other merchandise before I realized it. (By the way, if this happens to you call your credit card immediately to report it so you can minimize your liability for the purchases - I didn't have to pay anything but it was a pain to deal with anyway). So, it's up to you whether you want your real name on your books. Mark Twain wasn't his real name either - it was Samuel Langhorne Clemens.

A Sale-Generating Product Description

Your Product Description, the few paragraphs that describe your book on your Amazon product page, is really high in determining your book's success (perhaps behind SEO and writing a great book). It is your book's main advertisement, so I'm sure you can imagine just how important it is. When deciding whether to buy an Amazon book, you read the description of the book. Is it poorly written? Does it turn you off of buying the book? Do you read a powerful description of the book and think, "Wow - I have to buy this right now?" You have to remember that sales are made or die based on your product description.

My best advice is to check out the book descriptions of books that are selling well on Amazon (ranked 10,000 or less). You can even look at the top 10 to top 100 books on Amazon. The Top 100 Paid Books and Top 100 Free Books are listed on Amazon.com. What about the book descriptions make people buy the book? Are they using lots of action words (Buy Now) or power words (Killer, Amazing)? What keywords are they using? Is the book description written in first person by the author ("I wrote this book about bee mating habits because…) or third person ("Author Sue Grant, a researcher with twenty years of experience in raising bees, wrote this book to….").

All the advice I've heard from experts is to write the book description in the third person, as a traditional publisher would. I don't do this with my nonfiction books. I write them in the first person because I want my potential customers to feel as if I'm talking to them on a personal level. Again, I'm doing the opposite of what most experts say is successful, and doing so with excellent results. Ultimately, that decision is up to you. You might even use first person for one book description and third person for another. I have a few fiction works that I use third person for. Do whatever you think will be most effective in selling your book. You can always change it. You can change descriptions, price, categories, keywords, etc. within 12 to 24 hours on your books. You make the change, and within 12 hours or so (being in the US), the change will be evident on your product page.

Getting back to your product description, usually longer is better. There are several reasons for this. One is that the more words you use, the better chance your book has in showing up in different Amazon searches (because searches are based on keywords). However, don't stuff the descriptions with keywords - just add them in naturally or you will detract from your product description. Another reason that longer is better is that you have that much more time to try to convince the reader to buy. That's why longer TV commercials cost more than shorter ones - more time to convince the customer to purchase. You don't have to have a long, perfect product description from Day One. You can put up a description and improve upon it later on (remember changes show up in only about 12 hours in the US, a bit longer if you're not).

I also suggest that you break up your product description into several different paragraphs. When people see a huge block of text to read, they are more apt to skip it than to read it. However, if you start out with just a short paragraph or two, they will be more inclined to read it. It is less time consuming to read a short paragraph, it requires less commitment, and internet users have short attention spans. They like to zoom around a lot to maximize their experience.

Formatting Product Descriptions

You can also format your product page on Amazon. By using special formatting formulas (html), you can make your product description more appealing to customers. You can bold words, use italics, and change font size and color. Instead of using regular html, you have to use particular formatting. Amazon doesn't use regular html - it won't work. You have to have the special html to be able to bold, have colored fonts, sizes, and have it work on Amazon. This formatting is beyond the scope of this book, but I wanted to mention it in case you're interested in going that extra mile to format your product descriptions. If you're interested on specially formatting your Kindle product description, you can find books on the subject on Amazon.

Reviews - Make It or Break It

Reviews are absolutely crucial to the success of your ebook. Some sites that promote Kindle ebooks won't even accept submissions from you if you don't have at least 5 or 10 good reviews. Doing free book promotions on Amazon can help with this - I usually get at least a couple of reviews from my few promo days. Just so you know, very few readers leave reviews on Amazon. You can give away 1,000 books and not get a single review from that. Basically, you just have to wait and see - be patient. Some of my ebooks have been up for seven months and only have 18 reviews.

It's important to write a good book, because when you do get those important reviews, you certainly want them to be good ones. Positive reviews make people feel better about purchasing your book. They are more comfortable taking a chance on your book. Bad reviews will kill your book, so spend the time up front to make sure people will like your book. In the same token, however, realized that you will get some bad reviews. Some people just like to go around handing out bad reviews or trying to hinder your sales. Don't take it personally. Just keep moving forward. And don't respond to bad reviews – it just makes you look bad and unprofessional.

One thing you can do, which has helped me personally increase my number of reviews, is to ask your readers to leave a short review on Amazon if they've enjoyed your book. You do this at the end of each of your books. You can't ask for reviews on your Amazon product page (not allowed), but you can mention it within the text of your book. Also, you can't pay for Amazon reviews - don't risk your precious Amazon account by trying to beat the system. That is strictly against the rules. Make sure you read Amazon's terms of service - the whole thing - so you know what the rules are.

Marketing Strategies that Sell Books

As I mentioned previously, SEO (search engine optimization) is my main method of marketing my Kindle ebooks. If enough people can find your product page on Amazon via search engines (Google being the main one on the internet, and Amazon's search engine, of course), then you will get sales. You have to use the right keywords so find a keyword tool you like to find popular keywords – I currently like Merchantwords). Long-tail keywords (keywords containing 3 or more words) are the most effective. If you use "dogs" as a keyword, you're going to be pretty much competing with everyone with a dog-related book, site or blog. If you use "dog training", you've cut down on a lot of competition, but there will still be tons of it. If you go a step further and use "dog training manuals for small breeds," then you've cut down your competition even further. That's why long-tail keywords work better than short ones.

Just remember, those long-tail keywords must be showing a decent amount of searches per month on the Keyword Tool to make them profitable and worth using. I like keywords that have 10,000 searches a month or more.

Just type in a keyword (one or two words in length) that you want to check out and hit search. Again, we want keywords made up of at least 2 or 3 words, at least 10,000 searches a month (more is better), and low competition. Make a list of possible profitable keywords.

Head over to Amazon and use their website's search engine to look up the keywords on your list. Do the same keywords pop up under the search box (as suggestions Amazon gives you for your search)? If so, that's a really good sign. That means that a lot of people on Amazon are looking for those keywords as well. Next, take a look at the top books that come up for those keywords. We want to know if their sales volume is adequate to make it worth the time to write a book about this. Popular books will pop up first in the results that Amazon shows you. What is the rank on those books? Is it 20,000 or lower? If so, that's a book to consider writing. Continue your research until you have a few possibilities of books to write.

A word of wisdom - don't forget to do the research first! I've written at least one Kindle book that has dismal sales because I used just a Keyword tool. I thought it would be very popular, and spent time writing the book only for it to have very low sales. That's why you have to research first, using both the Keyword Tool and Amazon. I hate the fact that I wasted that time writing that particular book, but it was a learning experience. I won't make that mistake again. It was obviously a lesson I needed to learn.

Even if you aren't great at SEO at first, you can still make money with Kindle ebooks. I have some books that make enough to pay the monthly mortgage on my $250,000 home. I'd be more specific, but most big sites don't allow direct sales figures to be quoted. I have books that only make enough to buy a couple of pizzas a month. These include a couple fiction books I wrote for fun, and the one I forgot to research correctly. Even at this small amount, if I wrote 2 books a month, I could create about $480 a month passive income after a year. This would be 2 books times around $20 times 12 months. That's still pretty darn good if you ask me. (Obviously I can't guarantee this because every author and book is different, but it's certainly a reasonable assumption based upon my experience).

My other main marketing technique is the one I mentioned earlier - using the free promotion days that Amazon allows KDP Select books. If I have a struggling book, I will do a free promo for multiple days (3 to 5 in a row) in an attempt to improve its rank, and thus sales, on Amazon. Sometimes it's very successful, other times not as much - depending on how many people download the free book.

Advertising Your Kindle Book Free Days

The only other marketing I do is to sometimes advertise my ebook's free Kindle days on the sites I listed previously. Actually, I rarely do this because I don't really want to (lazy me - I'd rather be writing). I have outsourced this boring task to a person on Fiverr before (only once). I just usually forget to do it, so it's obviously not required. As far as downloads go, I believe the subject of the ebook is far more important than whether you advertised the free days of your ebook around the internet.

Here's why I believe this: The book I just gave away over 10,000 copies of was not advertised on any of the "kindle free ebook day" sites. I didn't bother to do it, and I gave away far more copies than I had for books that I did list on "kindle free ebook day" sites. For example, one book that I did advertise its free days was only downloaded about 1,000 times. Apparently, demand for a certain book's subject is far more important than anything else. That's really not surprising when you think about it - demand for the product is king (as usual). The book that was downloaded over 10,000 times had more of a broad appeal (more people were interested in the subject) than the other book did. Remember that demand for the product is king - always.

Keep On Writing Books

I continue to write at least a book or two every single month. I do this for several reasons. First of all, eventually sales for my existing books will drop off. However, word-of-mouth advertising is the most effective marketing in the world. There are over 300 million people just in the U.S.. My selling even 200 copies of one book a month only means around 2,400 people have bought it. That still leaves a whole lot of people out there to buy my book.

Still, sales will eventually drop off after the books have been around a while. I'm consciously preparing against this by constantly adding more books. These additional books will make up for any decrease in demand that occurs in the future. Eventually I'll have so many books that they will stabilize any individual book's decrease in demand. It's kind of like investing in mutual funds, which are made up of the stocks of many different companies. The diversification reduces risk, and the different stocks (in our case books) stabilizes the whole. Diversification makes our library of books less volatile in the face of changing demand.

I also add books monthly to make more money. I'm trying to increase my monthly residual income to a point where I don't have to work at anything and can spend my days however I want to. My goal would probably be about $10,000 a month residual income from Kindle books. I could definitely live quite nicely on that, given my husband's income as well. Using the skills I've acquired over the past few years, I expect this may take me two or three more years of writing and publishing. Not bad - forty years slaving away at a regular job or just a few years publishing. The real kicker is, I believe publishing to be much more profitable. I'm in control of how much money I make, not my employer.

The great thing about writing books is that the number of books I write is virtually limitless. I can write book after book, month after month, year after year. My income is only limited by my own ambition. As long as I'm around, I can write books and add to my residual income. I am literally creating my future, and even a future for my family. Some authors get a generational trust through an attorney so that their royalties go to their heirs after they die. All this residual income is a lot different than a regular job where "the powers that be" might decide to give you a measly 3% raise next year, if you're lucky. Through publishing, I've given myself around an 80% raise just within a few months.

Why I Love Publishing

The company you work for might decide to do away with your position, and tell you about it tomorrow. I've been laid off three times in my life - all through no fault of my own. Necessary budget cuts meant that positions had to be eliminated, and I was among the victims. The interesting thing I found out was that long after the unemployment checks stopped, the income from my online ventures kept flowing in. It allowed us to keep our home, our cars - everything. We got through, but only because of the money from my "side work" that I'd done for myself (not through my job) years before.

My safety net, our saving grace, was income from writing I'd done many years before. That's why I believe that working for yourself in this way is far more secure than working for someone else. As long as Amazon is around, I'm in good shape. I don't think they'll be going anywhere anytime soon. I read recently that Kindle book sales make more money for Amazon now than regular books do. I'll keep writing. It's just too much fun to have Amazon making deposits to my checking account every month.

That reminds me of one thing I should tell you. You won't actually get your first Amazon payment of royalties for a couple of months after you start making sales. Depending on what part of the month you start selling in, it will be two to three months before you get your first royalty payment. That's just the way it is. This is pretty traditional, actually. For the online course I wrote, I didn't get my first check for around two months. The good news is, once you wait the two or so months to get your first payment, you will get your royalty payment (provided you had sales) every month thereafter. You just have to get through that initial lag in the payment. I usually get paid on the 30th of the month via direct deposit.

Also, remember that you will need to withhold money to

pay your taxes as your royalties are taxable income. Speak to your accountant or tax expert first - depending on how much you make you may even have to make quarterly tax payments during the year to the IRS. I'm not a tax expert, and don't pretend to be - so go to your tax expert for advice and counsel on how you should deal with taxes on your royalties.

Amazon will currently let you set up your Amazon Kindle Publishing account as an individual, with your name and social security number. You should consult your tax expert and attorney about different business structures (sole proprietorship, LLC, Corporation) and their advantages and disadvantages in order to decide whether you should form a business or not, what type of business would work best for your individual situation, and how to form one if you so desire.

As for me, I've come to realize that I no longer care whether or not my job is eliminated. This is thanks to my online course and Kindle publishing royalties. I can take care of myself just as well, in fact better than, I did with my 'regular job.' I said earlier, I'm about to make the switch to becoming a publisher full-time and not working outside of the home at all. This has been a dream of mine for quite some time, and perhaps yours as well given that you're reading this book.

Why Most People Aren't Successful at Online Business

Many people try online businesses and fail. Why is this? I believe it's because the vast majority of people don't want to put in the necessary work to make their online business successful. Websites don't build themselves, and books don't write themselves. To make money, people have to put in the work. One way or another, you have to put in some effort, either physical or mental, to make money. You might not have to keep working forever, as is the case with publishing, but you will have to do the required tasks at some point. Somewhere along the line, probably because of all the 'make money without doing anything' hype and scams, many got the idea that an internet business is big money, no work.

If you have this notion, the sooner you let go of it the better. Have you ever heard the saying, "The more I work, the luckier I get"? That is absolutely true. Every time I've been successful creating a stream of income, I've done so by putting in the work. Do the necessary tasks, work hard, have faith, and you will get to where you want to be.

Conclusion

We've come to an end, my friend - you now know what I know about becoming a successful indie Kindle publisher. I hope you've learned a lot. I know it may seem overwhelming if you've never done anything like this before. Keep in mind that although I've been a publisher for five years, I've been writing online, studying SEO on the internet, and investigating ways to make money online for a lot longer than that. Don't get discouraged - take one step at a time. That's how progress is made - in baby steps. The major difference that sets winners apart is that winners will do things that other people don't want to. You have to be willing to give up whatever you're currently doing to work on this project. Give up the time you watch TV, Facebook, or surf the net. Instead, start researching book topics. Then, write your book. You don't have to finish it in a week - do it at your own pace. Keep moving forward, and I'm sure you'll be very happy with where you end up.

More Possibilities

Unlike some people who write about making money online, I actually do it. I haven't had a "regular job" since 2008. I'm a mother of two children with a college degree, but most of what I do online does not require a formal education. How much did I pay up front to make money online? Absolutely nothing. Making money online can be FREE – you just have to know where to go.

In this section, I'm going to share with you what I know about making money online, as well as some great additional resources I've found for finding legitimate part-time and full-time employment opportunities. We'll even discuss some other options that are out there for starting your own business online or from the comfort of your own home. I have included some options for people who do have a bit of start-up money. Keep in mind, though, that I have never paid anything up front to start making money online.

Everyone wants to work from home, don't they? Or if they don't, they should. I get up when I want, pick my kids up from school, make meals, do laundry, go to appointments, go shopping – basically spend my time as I like while making money. I absolutely will never work for anyone else again…ever.

Once upon a time, a long time ago, I worked in an office. I had my own cubicle, and made sales calls. It was draining, it was boring, and all the while I could only think of a way to get out of cubicle hell. I looked around at the people who had worked there for twenty or more years, and could see my future self in their worn faces…what a nightmare! Anyway, I got out!!! It definitely wasn't the easy road, but I wouldn't change a thing. I've never looked back!

What are the main obstacles to people who want to make money online fast – like now? Well, starting your own online business can be time-consuming and expensive. You might set up your own website (costs money for hosting, design, domain names), only to realize you have no visitors – like NONE. Then, you do lots of back-linking with articles from other sites and work like Hell to try to get traffic to your site. Believe me – I've done it. It's an uphill battle. That's when I discovered that you're much better off using sites that have been set up by professionals and already have millions of visitors. We'll talk about which sites these are and how you can use them to put money in your own pocket. There really are big companies out there who are willing to share the income with you.

And you do have some cards in your hand. One of the main advantages you have as an online worker is flexibility. At times, you'll discover a great way to make money online and then have the rug ripped out from under you. As I mentioned earlier, this has happened to me at least three times.

When a company like Amazon makes changes, I have to

adjust and change what I write and publish, decide whether to partake in borrowing systems they offer to customers, and so on. Businesses are alive, changing creatures and you have to be willing to adjust or be left in the dust. Also, remember that it is best to diversify your income online when you can – as any of the sites you use for income can change the rules at any time.

Microworkers/Microjobs

Some sites will allow you to sign up for free as a worker and then perform small tasks or jobs online in order to make money. The tasks are usually pretty simple, so the pay is often small per task. However, if you find a certain type of task that you don't mind doing and can do quickly, they can add up fast. Let's take a few moments to discuss some of these.

Mechanical Turk

I tried this one recently as well (after hearing someone say they were making money there) – the jobs (simple tasks) pay little (cents) and for most people there are easier ways to make money online. I felt I was spending too much time looking for the jobs to do rather than actually working and getting paid for it. Remember – time is money! Still, it's free to use – you just have to sign up. If you can stay focused and find some easy tasks that you can do quickly, it might be the place for you.

www.mturk.com

Crowdsource

This is another micro-task site where workers are trained and tested, and then qualified workers can choose tasks from their catalog of work to complete for clients, which they are then paid for. Tasks can include things like writing, calling a business for information, or creating a new topic for a discussion board, among others of course.

www.crowdsource.com

Youtube.com

It's free to post videos to Youtube, obviously, because everyone and their brother seems to have videos on there. Some are informational, some are ridiculous. So, you post some how-to videos, enable advertising on them, and then bring in between $1 to $3 per 1,000 views on Youtube. More videos means more overall views, so load lots of videos on a desired topic, and build your viewership by developing a following. Again, check out www.youtube.com to see what video topics are popular with viewers. Youtube is very popular and there are many people making a killing there in terms of income. Just take a look at the number of views some videos are getting and when they were put up. That will give you an idea how much money some youtubers are making on their videos. Yes, some people are making thousands a month on their youtube videos.

Youtube is my new project – I've just created my first video that I will be uploading in the very near future – probably as soon as I publish this ebook!

To make my videos myself, I use MovieMaker (part of Windows Essentials) – it's very easy to add pictures, music, and voiceovers to it, and the download for it is even free! I taught myself to use it and was up and running, making my first video that very night. Remember to read Youtube's Terms of Service prior to even starting to make your videos, as they are very strict about licensing and making you prove you have the rights to use any pictures, soundtrack, and content in your videos. You don't want to lose your account before you even get started! Ouch!

Teach Online

Lots of companies hire people to teach online. There are many opportunities. You can apply to adjunct online for any of the universities that offer online courses. SNHU is just one of the many colleges that offer such opportunities. Check out individual sites to find out whether you qualify to teach online for them. Some of the large online universities are Kaplan, American Public University, and University of Phoenix.

Adjunctprofessoronline.com offers all kinds of resources for adjunct professors as well as job listings by state. Many of these jobs require some time on campus, so they are not 'online jobs' per se. However, if you have some teaching experience and the required formal education, you can check with both traditional colleges and newer 100% online colleges for possible online job openings.

I've taught online for almost twenty years, so I know there are lucrative, real opportunities out there if you can find them, apply, and get hired.

Edtech is very popular right now – finding education solutions using technology. There are sites like Udemy where you can create your own course and share the revenue with them in exchange for them hosting your course on their platform. Or, you can host the course yourself. There are lots of options out there when you're looking to create and sell an online course.

Skillshare

Skillshare is another way to teach online. You record a bunch of videos showing how you do something, and take part in forums related to your class. In return, you get a portion of the money from the people who sign up for your class. There site says average pay for instructors averages $3500 per year. This might be an option for you if you just need a little extra cash per month. No teaching experience required, they have 1,000 teachers and a million students.

www.skillshare.com

Virtual Assistants

Virtual assistants (VA) or virtual office assistant is defined as a generally self-employed person who provides professional administrative, technical, or creative (social) assistance to clients remotely from a home office (Wikipedia.com). If you're good with organization, making reservations, and administrative tasks, this could be the business for you.

If you're thinking of becoming a virtual assistant, here are some sites that may be of help to you!

Assistu.com offers training for virtual assistants as well as a registry so clients can find them. Some services on the site cost money, but you don't necessarily need to purchase training or placement in a registry to start a business as a virtual assistant.

IVAA.org is the professional organization for virtual assistants, if you're interested.

So, how to do this for free and get a lot of traffic to your virtual assistant listings? You could use Fiverr.com to offer services to customers (Example: I will work as a virtual assistant for you for 30 minutes for $5, and then use the gig-extras to offer other services for higher amounts of money).

You may want to eventually set up an upwork.com (formerly elance.com) profile as a virtual assistant. You can set up a free Freelancer account there.

Zirtual.com

Another option for budding virtual assistants is Zirtual. Interested in working full-time, every day, as a virtual assistant? Sign up to be a Zirtual assistant to someone who's busy…and needs help. You would do research, handle emails, reservations, organization – basically any assistant tasks in exchange for the base pay which starts at $11 per hour. Employment opportunities with them are highly competitive – applicants undergo testing in many areas and they only hire 1 to 2% of people who apply to them.

www.zirtual.com

Upwork

Upwork, formerly Odesk, which also purchased Elance, is now a huge freelancer site. Over a billion dollars worth of work is done annually on Upwork, so that should give you an idea of the money to be made there. All different kinds of freelancers, from writers to software developers, offer their services on this site. Businesses use it to hire professionals to perform all sorts of jobs. In fact, Upwork is very popular for both individuals and businesses looking to hire freelancers of all kinds. I've hired people from Upwork to design logos for me and do other business-related tasks in the past. If you're interested, check out their Terms of Service. They charge a service fee for freelance work done on the site as of this writing as well as membership programs.

www.upwork.com

Making Money Online – Another Option for Writers

Another good option would be Hubpages, where you post articles (if you're smart you will do keyword research to decide which topics to write articles about). Hubpages merged Squidoo into it, so it is now one of the largest networks of what is considered amateur content online. You are paid a portion of the Google Adsense and Amazon Affiliates income from ad clicks from the advertisements on or in between your posted articles. No upfront cost to you, and you can add more and more articles every day. This is great passive income, but don't expect to get rich overnight. Expect to write articles and build your income overtime. How much will you make? It depends – but the better you are at picking lucrative keywords, the more you will make. Some writers on the site are reporting monthly incomes of close to $1000 while others make only a couple hundred a month (or less). You can register for Hubpages today and get started building your empire!

Find a Part-Time Job Online

A few years ago, I needed to make some extra income. By finding a listing on an online database, I found a job writing articles for an international company and posting them online. It definitely helped me earn some extra easy money to get me through a rough spot. I did it for a few months until I found some better options for myself that would allow me to make more money on my own online. Still, if you want to work on the side from home and get some income coming in, you might want to consider getting a part-time online job.

These next few listings are free databases you can use to find part-time or full-time work on or off-line

Flexjobs

Flexjobs.com is a great resource for finding telecommuting jobs and opportunities. You've got to love a site that spends the time to hand-screen every job so you don't have to waste time on scams. These are all levels of jobs (professional), with flexible work options, that are legitimate, and they offer a satisfaction guarantee as well. So, this is definitely on the list to check out. I'm sure you'll be surprised at the many reputable companies that allow flexible work arrangements. There is no fee for searching their database. Here's the link for it www.flexjobs.com .

Indeed.com

At Indeed.com, you can put in your zipcode and see the current, real jobs available in your area – part-time, full-time, and otherwise. State Labor departments refer people to Indeed.com to find jobs – so there are many good postings there for real jobs (not all are online opportunities, but if you need to find a part-time or full-time job, check it out). As always, use your common sense – scammers can slip in anywhere so if it sounds too good to be true, it probably is. www.indeed.com

Simplyhired.com

Simplyhired is another online job database that allows you to search for available positions online and offline in your area. Real local jobs that are available in your area. Check it out if you get the chance! Today, there's not just Monster.com for finding jobs. www.simplyhired.com

Care.com

If you want to care for children, the elderly, or do errands for people such as shopping, this is the place to go. You need to register in order to see the jobs, but it is an easy process. Just create a free profile and search for jobs at Care.com. You can search for local opportunities that might just fit in perfectly to your needs and schedule.

If you're looking for a part-time job, ask around to see about opportunities for helping an elderly client in their home. I have a friend who works for an elderly woman, helping her with meals, laundry, transportation, and just keeping her company for around 20 hours a week. She gets paid about $10 an hour, and it works out great for both of them. There are many elderly people who want desperately to stay in their own homes with just a bit of help and company from someone a few hours a day or week.

www.care.com

Swagbucks

If you don't mind getting paid in gift cards from Target, Amazon, Itunes, etc. then you may like Swagbucks, which is probably the most popular and legitimate survey site out there. You can do several of these consumer surveys a day, and companies use the information to make product decisions. I wouldn't expect to get rich from doing surveys and getting paid if gift cards, but if you have an inclination to do this, go ahead…

Linkshare

Linkshare is now owned by Rakuten, and it is a company that allows you to put links to their sponsor's products on your websites or blogs. You get paid a commission whenever anyone follows that link and purchases a product. Lots of famous companies like Walmart are involved with Linkshare now, so finding good products and companies to advertise for is not difficult. You do have to apply to work with them, but I didn't have any trouble with regard to that so I don't think it's too difficult. You make commissions so there are no upfront expenses paid to Linkshare.

Linkshare is another one of my projects. I picked one company that offers about 300 different products, and have built affiliate links with my Linkshare code to send traffic to that company. This is a relatively new project for me, and is just starting to gain some traction. I expect it to grow into a substantial income in the future.

CJ Affiliate by Conversant

Formerly Commission Junction, this online advertising company operates worldwide in what is referred to as the affiliate marketing industry. Publishers get approved by the company to be affiliate marketers for their clients in exchange for a commission on sales. Big companies like QVC and Expedia are clients for this site. There are lots of other affiliate marketing companies such as Linkshare and CJ Affiliate as well.

www.cj.com

Stock Photography

Like to take photos? Thousands of new blogs and websites are started every day, and site owners need photos for those sites. There are many sites where you can earn money for your photos that are downloaded by customers.

Some of the popular stock photography sites are

istockphoto, shutterstock, dreamstime, and crestock. Pay varies, with some paying 20% of the downloaded price and others paying $.25 and up per picture. Photos can be downloaded over and over again, so if you put up a lot of great pictures, the income can really add up.

I will include additional stock photography sites in the Resources section at the end of this ebook.

Start a Service Business Online – Not FREE but an Interesting Idea

I live in a small town, and I have a friend who started a concierge business. She finds contractors for individuals or businesses including but not limited to house cleaners. She has a wide array of contractors that she trusts to do work such as painting and cleaning, opening camps, etc. She saves people time by doing various tasks such as errands and paperwork that they don't want to have to handle on their own. This young woman made over $100,000 last year. She has a website that lists the different kinds of projects that she coordinates and the kind of contractors she can hire for clients. In addition to her online presence, she also gets great word-of-mouth advertising from her many happy customers. Even including the cost of an inexpensive website, this kind of service business can be relatively low-cost to start.

I realize that some of you may be interested in selling products online. For you, I have included the following resources that may help you get started. Costs will vary.

Finding Manufacturing or Products that You Can Resell – May Require Money Upfront

Thinking of selling a product? Amazon is a great place to sell products, simply because of the amount of traffic that the website receives. Can you imagine the work you'd have to put in for years and years in order to push that many people to your own personal website? It would simply never happen. To sell on Amazon, you'd need a product to sell. Check out www.thomasnet.com (the official online presence for Thomas's Register for Manufacturers). This database is full of contract manufacturers for all kinds of different products from clothing to food. If you're looking for a manufactured product to resell, here's the real database you've been looking for.

If you're interested in selling online, another new option is Alibaba.com – China's answer to Amazon. www.alibaba.com

Dropshippers

Don't want to handle product and hold inventory for your online business? You can find companies which will dropship their product to your customers once they place an order with you. Check out www.worldwidebrands.com to learn how to find manufacturers who will drop-ship to customers for you. Many people who make a lot of money selling products on Amazon use dropshippers. This often prevents you from having to purchase inventory up front as well.

Be careful because there are tons of fake dropshipper sites out there – basically companies that claim to be wholesale dropshippers, but they really aren't. Their prices are too high – not wholesale at all. There is no way you can make money doing this because you are buying product at too high a price to resell at a profit. Also, there are so many people who fall victim to this kind of fake dropshipping site that you will find the same products being sold by multiple people online (at sites like Ebay, for example).

Before picking any product to sell online, make sure you can buy it for about half of what you can sell it for. This will take some online research, but don't just go blindly into things. Look the product you are thinking of selling up on various sites like Ebay and Amazon, even Target and Walmart – to make sure that customers are willing to buy the product for your targeted selling price.

Depending upon the dropshipper you go with, you may not have to pay any money upfront.

FBA – Fulfillment by Amazon is another option you may want to look into if the idea of finding products to sell, sending them to Amazon and selling these products on the site appeals to you. I don't personally do this, but I know a lot of entrepreneurs who do and make a killing doing it. There are a lot of videos on youtube if you'd like to learn more about it.

Flipping Sites – An Option Once You Have Some Money to Invest

Flippa is a website where sites and domains are bought and sold online. If you're interested in purchasing a site that's already made and getting income from Adsense or Affiliate marketing, you might want to check that out. For an upfront investment, you can purchase a site that potentially could bring in one or more streams of income. Take your time to look around and learn as much as you can about a site before purchasing, of course. Make sure you see income reports that are very recent and know what will be required by you to keep the income at that level prior to purchase. Check rankings, such as the Alexa ranking, of any sites you are considering.

As with any investment, you need to do your due diligence (lots of careful research) before investing in anything – including a website. I know one man who spent $5000 on a website and recouped 50% of that investment within the first year of running the site himself. After approximately another year, given this return on investment rate, he will have regained his investment and all other income from the site will be pure profit. He owns several sites, of course, and has found it to be a better option than creating his own sites for profit. This is because building a site, determining good keywords, creating content, and driving traffic to it can take a year or longer. Another site that is like flippa in terms of format is www.empireflippers.com. Sites range in price, with ones that make more money selling for higher prices than lower profit sites, of course. I've purchased websites from Flippa before that make money with Adsense advertising, and it is something I plan to expand upon in the future.

www.Flippa.com

(Another option, of course, is to develop websites and sell them on flippa or a site like it.)

Beware of Scams – As Always!

I just read a fake article on what looked like a legitimate news site about a woman named Mary Stevens (who lives in my area) making $8000 a month posting links for sites like Google, Amazon, etc. After looking carefully at the check, which was purposely blurred, I realized it was not the correct area/address on the check. The accompanying picture of "Mary Stevens" looked like a stock photo of a young woman and her baby. Upon further investigation online, I found this is just one of the latest scams that are fooling people all over the internet, and stealing their money from them.

Always investigate any questionable enterprise before giving anyone your credit card number. Simply type the name of the product or service and the word "scam" into Google, and see what other people have to say about it. Better safe than sorry!

For all the ways I've made money online including Ehow, Hubpages, Google Adsense, Amazon KDP, teaching online, and so on, I have NEVER paid for the privilege to do so. Sure, you do pay these companies in terms of sharing earnings with them, but you shouldn't have to pay anything upfront. In fact, I'd be wary of any company that wants you to pay them a fee to make money with them.

Decide What's Best for YOU

There are a lot of ways to make real money online for free

– we've covered many of them. I think most important of all is finding something that seems to fit you. Some people like sales and would be more suited to selling products on Amazon, while others who have writing and publishing ability may do better publishing ebooks. If you prefer to find an opportunity where you can get a job helping an elderly person in your area, check out Care.com online for listings and to leave a profile. If you're looking for a remote working job or telecommuting, you may find what you need on one of the free job sites I've provided for you. If you find something that suits you, then you will be more likely to stick with it and be successful.

The difference between people who are successful at making money online and those who aren't is that the successful ones are willing to go the extra mile. The internet isn't super-easy money (like some people imagine) – you have to sell a product or service, whether its ebooks or advertising or toasters. You have to do the work – you need to find something profitable and do the work to get your money-making business set up. Start small and work your way into something big. If you aren't willing to do the work, you won't be able to make money online. It's just as simple as that. Set yourself apart from the masses by actually taking the steps you need to in order to make it.

Point to remember: Pick projects that you are interested in and that you personally feel you can be successful with!

Getting Started

People often ask me how I got started making money online, and I tell them to take it one step at a time. Research Amazon and come up with an idea for an ebook you could write, and start on page one. Work on that a little each day until you have a completed one, and then publish. Even if you only make $100 on your Amazon sales, that's still an extra $100 a month. It's very easy to make $100 a month on Fiverr.com, if you pick popular gigs to offer. That would be an extra $200 a month. And you're just starting out.

My first month teaching online, I made about $100 – because I didn't have a lot of students at that point. This month, that income was $2200. My first month selling ebooks on Amazon, I only made around $300, which I thought was excellent at the time. I obviously make much, much more than that now. It takes work, and you have to grow your projects, adding additional residual income streams along the way. (Residual income is income that comes in automatically after you have set it up – the very best kind of income).

The secret to making money online is to build it up from scratch – you start at nothing, but add to it a little at a time. Each project should increase your monthly online income, and once you finish one project, you need to move on to the next. In this book, I've given you all the possibilities I know of in terms of ways to make money online (different possible projects). One you begin to see some good income coming in, you may then want to try investing in one of the money making opportunities that require a cash outlay – such as buying Adsense sites, for example. If you find something that's successful for you, do more of it!

Whenever possible, try to diversify your online income – just in case any one source of income pulls the rug out from under you. You need something else – preferable many "something elses" to be able to rely upon.

Conclusion

It looks like we've reached the end of this ebook, but your journey making money online is just beginning. If you're looking for extra income as soon as possible, Textbroker or Fiverr.com are good choices. You can write articles as soon as you are approved on Textbroker. You can put up your gigs on Fiverr as soon as you register - for FREE - and start working as soon as you get an order. Amazon Kindle Direct Publishing is also fast to get started (and FREE with no upfront costs)– you can start writing your book today and publish as soon as it's completed. With Amazon, there is about a two month lag in payment (for example, the deposit I get on in the end of March 2017 is for my January sales). However, once you get started, you will be getting a check or direct deposit at the end of every month. Still, if you need money right now, you might want to take that into consideration and look for something that will pay faster.

If you're looking for a part-time job for extra money, check out those job sites I gave you – Care.com, Indeed, Flexjobs, etc. Once you get hired, you should have a relatively fast pay day. For those of you who have the extra time to dedicate and perhaps some upfront funds (you may not need any upfront money, depending on the specific opportunity you choose, whether your supplier will give you net 30 terms for payment, etc.), you may want to look into what it would take to set up sales of a product (maybe using a dropshipper) on Amazon or Alibaba (the huge company that is the "Amazon" of China). These sites get tons of traffic and if you can find a high demand product, you'll be well on your way to becoming successful online.

Making money online doesn't have to cost a lot – or anything at all to get started. Fiverr and Amazon KDP are just two examples of online businesses that are willing to share the riches with you. Check out opportunities that you're interested in, and then find a way to make them work. Best of luck to you in your online money-making adventures! And check out the Resources I've listed below – just for you!

Best of luck to you, and remember – in this world, we make our own luck!

RESOURCES FOR YOU

For Writers – Start for FREE

www.IWriter.com

– you write articles and can earn $50 to $70 per week

www.kdp.amazon.com

Amazon Kindle Direct Publishing – publish your own original works and sell them on Amazon

For Local Job Seekers – FREE Sites and Databases to Use

www.monster.com

www.indeed.com

www.simplyhired.com

www.flexjobs.com

www.care.com

For Retailers

www.amazon.com

www.alibaba.com

www.worldwidebrands.com

www.thomasnet.com

For Buying and Selling Websites

www.flippa.com

www.empireflippers.com

For Site Builders and Bloggers

www.tumblr.com

www.blogger.com

www.wordpress.com

www.livejournal.com

www.blog.com

www.constant-content.com

For Teachers / Instructors

www.udemy.com

www.skillshare.com

www.phoenix.edu

www.kaplanuniversity.edu

www.apus.edu

For Affiliate Marketers

www.affilate-program.amazon.com

www.cj.com

www.maxbounty.com

www.clickbank.com

For Micro Workers

www.clickchores.com

www.microworkers.com

www.mturk.com

For Stock Photography

www.istockphoto.com

www.shutterstock.com

www.photostockplus.com

www.crestock.com

www.bigstockphoto.com

www.dreamstime.com

www.en.fotolia.com

www.123rf.com

MY BONUS FOR YOU – MY BOOK ON ACHIEVING SUCCESS IN LIFE

Think Your Way to Success

What is Success?

What does success mean to you? Although it seems quite simple and straight-forward, when you think about it success can mean many different things to many different people. Is success money? Is success fame? Is it both? For many, money is success and they have no interest in fame. Other people want to be rich and famous. Some people want to be rich, but don't want anyone to even know who they are. They would rather remain anonymous, in the background. Others want their names up in lights. These are two very different goals. Some individuals want to run their own business and everything that entails. Others want income, but no specific daily responsibilities. For some, success means only doing something that they love. So, the very first step in becoming successful is to think clearly about what success means to you. We must know the destination in order to begin the journey.

You've Got to Work

The only place where success comes before work is in the dictionary. Vidal Sassoon

Success does not come easily. Success takes a plan, and requires research, putting together the right people, and hard work. Sometimes you can substitute working smarter for working harder, but one way or another you have to work – mentally, physical, but usually both. Sometimes, when we look at people we consider successful, we think they were just lucky. Chances are, if you were to go back and look at what preceded their success, you would find a lot of effort in one form or another.

I've had some great successes in my life. I can tell you that none of them came without work, none came without some kind of journey that led to the ultimate goal being achieved. Be prepared to put in effort if you want to be successful. It's the only way.

I've had four major successes in my life. I consider a major success for me as one that brought in over $100,000 in income to me. Two were products I developed and then sold the rights to. The other two were projects that I put together – one a real estate project and the other a consultation agreement. I can tell you that each and every one of them required work – an idea, research, making the right connections, more work, and execution of the plan. Good things can happen in life, but they don't occur spontaneously on their own.

You've Got to Ask

In finding a project to follow up his Thriller album success, Michael Jackson tried to find a way to one-up himself – and Thriller was a very hard act to follow. Here's a list of ideas that were reportedly turned down: a Whitney Houston collaboration, a Barbara Streisand collaboration, a sing –off "fight" with Prince to see who was 'baddest,' done to the song "Bad". All evidently turned him down on these ideas. But, he went on to have huge hits like Black and White and Leave Me Alone, which he got a Grammy for. After that, he did the alien-inspired Scream, with his sister Janet, which hit Top 5.

Rich, super successful people get turned down too – we all do. It's part of life. You ask, you see if someone is interested in a project or not, and move on. You find another option, you find another way to proceed. If you hear no and quit, you will never be successful. That's a guarantee.

The internet makes making contacts extremely easy. Everyone has an email, a Facebook, and a twitter account. Say you read a book about a particular subject and you have a question about what the author says in the book. You can email them and ask a question or clarify something. If you have a project or an idea or collaboration, again you can contact them. Granted, if you contact celebrities, you probably either won't get an answer or just a courtesy one written by their assistant. However, if you contact people who aren't famous, you'll be surprised just how many of them are willing to talk to you. If you never ask, you'll never know. No one likes to be turned down, but the worst they can say is No. Often, you have to get a lot of No's to get one Yes.

You've Got to Put it Out There

Good things come to those who wait, but better things come to those who go and get them. **Anonymous**

Fortune sides with him (or her) who dares. Virgil

Do you have an idea for a product or even a prototype? Do you know how many people have ideas, ones they've even taken to the next step and developed into a product, but they're afraid to tell or show it to anyone? Guess what happens to those inventions, product ideas, and book concepts? Absolutely nothing! They never see the light of day because the person who came up with the idea is too afraid to put it out there. The idea dies with the person who was too afraid to do anything with it.

Granted, there is risk associated with showing or telling someone else your idea. Of course you should do your due diligence to make sure – at least as much as possible – that you are dealing with a reputable organization or individual. Document everything with pictures, copyrights, trademarks and even emails to show that you had original ownership and when. In the end, though, you have to be willing to do something with your idea if you ever expect to find success with it.

Most people who haven't developed product ideas think that the hardest part is thinking of the idea – the invention. In reality, that's the easy part. The hard part is finding the right organization to bring your idea to fruition. You have to develop a prototype, hook up with the right people, convince them that your idea is marketable and can ultimately be profitable. Then there's manufacturing and distribution to deal with. This all can take years and years. The idea is just the very beginning of the journey.

You've Got to Start Somewhere

Success is the sum of small efforts, repeated day-in and day-out. Robert Collier

Any journey, no matter whether it's a thousand miles (or less or more), starts with a single step. We're all super busy. It's very easy to put something off until we have the time to do it. Guess what? There won't ever be a good time to start. There's always something that will interfere or give us an excuse to wait. If we always put off until tomorrow, then tomorrow will never come. You must start, you must do something, in order to succeed.

If you've always wanted to write a book, you start with just a single word. You add to it, a little each day, until you have completed your project. Once that project is completed, then you have a finished product that you can do something with. You can pitch it to a traditional publisher, or you can publish it yourself in order to bring in additional personal income. Without that first word, you will get absolutely nowhere.

You'd be amazed how many times people put off things they want to do and then simply never get them done. They never know if that thing would have been a success, because they never tried it. They never got started. Don't be one of those people. Just taking those first steps and moving forward, a little at a time, will set you a part from the masses who will never even start.

Pick Yourself Up by Your Bootstraps

Little minds are tamed and subdued by misfortune; but great minds rise above it.

Washington Irving

I have a Master's degree in Business from a prestigious university. I graduated in the top of my class. I've headed departments and had thirty or more people working for me at any one time. I've been laid off five times! Crappy economies are harsh!

Anyway, each and every time, you have to lick your wounds, say, "Wow – that sucked!" and start thinking of your next move. You can't get stuck, and you can't succumb to negative thinking like:

I'll never find another job like that one.

No one will ever hire me again.

I'm going to go broke!

Or, even worse…

I must be a bad employee.

I'll never make it.

I am worthless.

You are most certainly not a bad employee or worthless. You can't take a lay-off or someone eliminating your department as a personal affront. It is a business decision – not a personal one. In fact, every time I was laid off, my boss felt terrible and offered me an excellent reference and even assistance in finding another position.

Things work out best for those who make the best of how things work out. John Wooden

My aunt got fired, due to necessary cuts, from a company she worked for for thirty years – since she graduated from high school. She literally went into shock, and then went home crying to her husband. Luckily, he had the clarity of mind to tell her, "Don't worry…it's just a job – you'll get another one." She did get another position, rather quickly, and she enjoys this one much more than the one she was fired from. She has been there over ten years now, and will likely stay there until she retires.

So, you got fired – pick yourself up, dust yourself off, and MOVE ON....

Success is walking from failure to failure with no loss of enthusiasm. Winston Churchill

Everyone has had bad times – you hear many accounts of very successful people who lost everything or filed for bankruptcy before finally making it. In fact, many of these people found that the third or fourth time they started a business was the charm. You just need to watch commercials to see that CareOne Debt Relief Services founder Bernie Dancel went bankrupt twenty years ago. In the face of adversity, it's important to remember that you're not the only one who's ever faced difficult circumstances. It helps you to keep the proper perspective.

You may have to fight a battle more than once to win it. Margaret Thatcher

The most important thing in life to remember is that we are all on a journey, and it's a journey that differs from anyone else's journey on the face of this planet. Any setback you encounter is not the end of the journey; it's just a bump in the road. Your journey will not be over until your last breath.

Many times, in the face of adversity, we think it's all over. It's not! Success requires that you keep going. What you just did didn't work, so now it's your job to find something that will.

You Need to Focus

Take up one idea. Make that one idea your life - think of it, dream of it, live on that idea. Let the brain, muscles, nerves, every part of your body, be full of that idea, and just leave every other idea alone. This is the way to success. Swami Vivekananda

We become what we think about most of the time, and that's the

strangest secret. Earl Nightingale

Now we're going to talk about focus.

Focus is defined as *the center of interest or activity.*

Another definition is *to pay particular attention to.*

Finally, although this definition refers to sight, it is also surprisingly applicable*:*

Focus is the state or quality of having or producing clear visual definition.

Any or all of these definitions of focus will work for us. Focus means that you come up with one idea or project to pursue to success and focus on it to the exclusion of all other ideas or projects at this time. You must make this project the center of your interest and your activity. You must pay particular attention to your project on a daily basis. You must do something each and every day to push your project along - whether that be writing, research, making contacts, etc. Finally, you must produce a clear, visual definition of what success with that project would look like to you. Keep that vision in your mind's eye. Think of it often, even daily. Don't stop until you've made that vision a reality in your life.

It's Your Time, Control It

If you don't value your time, neither will others. Stop giving away your time and talents- start charging for it. Kim Garst

You really get a sense of how **time is money** once you find a way to make money successfully. Before that, you're just messing around, trying a little bit of this and a little bit of that. It doesn't matter how much time you waste, or how much of your time other people waste. However, once you find a way to make money with what you do in your time, you realize that every little distraction is costing you.

Opportunity cost is a management term. Basically, it means

that the cost of doing something is really the loss of the potential gain you would have received if you'd done the alternative. So, if I mess around all week instead of doing work that would have brought in an extra $200 per month, then the cost of messing around this one week is $2400 per year.

That's why it's important to find a way to successfully make money – then you can put a value, at least in your mind, into what all your wasted hours are costing you.

Once we realize how valuable time is, you realize how important it is that you waste as little as possible on your road to success. Whenever you're doing something, whether it be checking your email, facebooking, checking out twitter, honestly ask yourself if this is really furthering you along on your journey to success. Chances are, the answer is NO. Be productive with your time, and not just pretending to be busy.

I have a cousin that used to live in his car when he was 20. He just sold his company for over ten million dollars. You hear stories like this and wonder whether things like this really happen. I can assure you they do. How did he go from homeless to rich and retired? I'll tell you.

He had drive. He started at the bottom of a large company, and they recognized his potential and sent him to college. The owner of a division of the large company really liked him and admired his motivation. He worked his way up in the company. When the owner retired, he sold his portion of this large company to my cousin. My cousin later sold his portion of the company, and retired a very rich man.

One time, he was in town and came to stay with me for a couple of days. I was struck by how productive this guy was. He was on the phone all night – with his accountant, business associates – he must've made twenty different phone calls. And he wasn't just chatting – he was giving direction telling each and every one of them what he needed or wanted done. That was when I realized that some people really are different – and apparently being very productive leads to success and great wealth. It may not happen overnight; his career lasted over twenty years. However, being highly productive certainly can't hurt. How productive are you on a daily basis? I had to ask myself that question, and make changes accordingly.

Get Organized

You need to make better use of your time and get more done – and thus make more money, if that is your idea of success. We've talked about focus. It's hard to focus if you are seated in the midst of chaos. Before starting on your pathway, the first step may be to get your environment under control. Put aside other projects for now. Make a clear workspace for yourself. You have to have somewhere where you can work without being interrupted. Make it as pleasant as possible – a workplace where you don't want to be won't be particularly productive.

Unfortunately, I can't give you a specific blueprint for getting organized because I'm not aware of each of your individual circumstances. Let's suffice it to say clean out the clutter, file and put away any other unnecessary projects you've been considering, and create a pleasant work environment for yourself.

Save Money

Not every opportunity takes money. Sometimes, a good idea and a bit of creativity in how you can go about it, is enough. Others times, however, you may need a little bit of funding, or even more. The importance of saving money becomes glaringly apparent at times like these.

Look around at all the possessions in your life. How many did you purchase for $20, $50, $100, or more? How often are you using these things? This is another MBA technique. Divide what you paid for an item by the amount of times you use it. That tells you whether it was a good value for you to buy it.

For example, I like a certain pair of shoes. I wear them every day and replace them when necessary. They aren't overly expensive – about $40. I have been wearing the current pair I have for two years. $40 divided by 730 days (in 2 years) equals .0547945. So, those shoes cost me about five cents a day or per use. I have purchased other shoes in the past for $40 or so, and never worn them. If I ever do decide to wear them once, they will cost me $40 for that one use. Not such a great deal at all.

In our society, we are always buying things we don't need or won't use. It also seems like people are always short on money. Start thinking about what you purchase. I believe it was Ben Franklin who used to say that the best way to double your money is to fold it in half and put it back in your pocket instead of spending it.

Some things are good investments. A comfortable bed will last you for years. I have a living room lamp I've had and used for at least the past twenty years. Use what you already have in order to save money. We live in a society that is designed to part us from our funds – that's what capitalism is all about. Don't fall into that trap. Save your money, have a bit of a cushion to not only fall back on in hard times but to also be able to use to invest in your future and your dreams.

Write Down What You Want

There's something about writing things down that makes them more concrete. I would like to encourage you to make a list of three to five things that you want in your life. You must write them down, as specifically as possible, and also in the present tense (as if they were already happening). This will help to imprint these goals in your mind, including your subconscious.

Here are a couple of examples:

I make $_____ per year.

I have my dream job working

_____.

I'm not sure why or how this works, but I know it has worked for me. Achievement of your goals won't happen overnight, but having specific, concrete goals somehow helps in your ability to attain them.

Make a Success Vision Board

Along the same lines, I encourage you to make a vision board of what success means to you. You can find pictures on the internet of things that appeal to you – bags of money, fancy cars, an attractive mate (if that's what you're looking for), or anything else. This is individualized – your personal vision. You can cut and paste these images into a document and print it out.

Another option would be to buy some poster board and cut out pictures in magazines or from the internet and glue them on. Put it above your desk at home or by the bureau next to your bed. Again, we are creating a clear vision of your success for your life. Look at it often.

Do Your Research

What you don't know really can hurt you. Somewhere out there is the means to your success in life. Until you find it, you will not have the success that you so desperately seek. That's how what you don't know can hurt you. Research what it will take for you to be successful. Do you want to start a business? Develop a product? Just find a way to successfully make money each and every day? Are you looking for your dream career? Any and all of these require a great deal of research. Set aside time each day to research your goal and the steps you would need to take to achieve it.

Try New Things

Opportunities don't happen, you create them. Chris Grosser

I just recently learned graphic design and desktop publishing in order to further my business. I read books related to my industry all the time. Books are great because you can learn a great deal for a small price. Even if I only learn one thing that helps with my endeavors, reading the book has been worthwhile. Knowledge and information are power. They increase your options. Now, I could use my new skills to make even more money by doing work for others – if I chose to do so.

Never stop learning. Gaining knowledge doesn't stop when you graduate from high school or college. The more you learn, the sooner you will find your way to success. You don't need to recreate the wheel. Chances are, someone else has already done what you want to do. Seek out that information and skip yourself ahead on the learning curve.

Try to Add Value

Successful entrepreneurs are givers and not takers of positive energy. Anonymous

The most successful business owners are ones who add value for their customers. If you can offer people a product or service that fulfills a need that they have, then you will be successful. You can't create demand, but you don't need to. People have many wants and needs already. You only need to be able to come up with something that will make their lives easier or better in some way. People who seek to help others are often far more successful than those that only look as far as how to make their next dollar. Always keep the needs of others in the forefront of your brain – that is often the key to success.

Over-Deliver

Try to over-deliver in everything you do. If you have

clients, give them more than what they would expect. Don't you love it when you get more than you expected to? That's how you develop a large base of loyal customers. If you work for someone else, that's how you can get more responsibility and become promoted. A key method to success that is often overlooked is doing your best in whatever you do – and giving those you do work for more than they ever would have expected.

You will find in life that many, many people do only the minimum of what is needed or required. Doing more will set you apart from all of the others. The path to success is paved for those who will not only do the things that other people won't do, but who will do more than what is expected. Because it is so rare, your customers and clients will remember and appreciate the extra effort you put in for them.

So how do we over-deliver? Can you perform the service well, but deliver it faster than expected? Can you do a little bit more than what was agreed upon? If you sell something, is there a way you can include an extra little gift for your customer? It doesn't have to be extravagant – just a little something extra. Can you follow up with a personalized phone call to ensure satisfaction with the product or service? Doing the little extras will help you stand out.

Do Something for Yourself On the Side

For extra income, and added insurance, do something for yourself on the side. You can start a small business whether it's writing articles online to sell, writing a blog, or starting a traditional business such as sharpening knives. Not only will this bring additional income into your life, but the income will also be there if you ever were to lose your regular job (if you work outside of the home). Starting a business is extra effort at first, however, it also allows you to deduct work-related expenses and thus lower your taxes. Consult an attorney and tax accountant to ensure that your business is legal and set up properly.

Have a Back-Up Plan

To live a creative life, we must lose our fear of being wrong.
Anonymous

Bad things happen to all of us. Not everything in life is going to work out as planned. Try to think ahead of what could go wrong and how you're going to deal with it. Hope for the best, but plan for the worst. Success means being realistic and preparing for different scenarios ahead of time. When something screwy happens, you'll be glad you planned for it. Successful people know that things are going to get mucked up, and they are able to roll with the punches. Preparation may mean putting money aside for those times when things are tight, or it might mean having enough irons in the fire that when one thing takes a dive there are others to soften the blow. Sometimes, it means both. Whatever it means, have a back-up plan in the works.

Here's an example of a back-up plan that I've used before. When things are going well financially, I set up a home equity line of credit. I did this, just in case I might need extra money in the future. Later, when I got laid off, I was able to access this line of credit in order to hold me over until we were back on our feet again. At that point, I was able to pay the line of credit off. Obviously, you need home equity, good credit, and income to qualify for the home equity line of credit. That's why I set it up ahead of time. And, of course, you have to be able to pay it or you will lose your home. So, although it's not something I would recommend to everyone, it is an example of a back-up plan I've successfully used before.

In any case, it's always a good idea to have some kind of a back-up plan, whether it's savings, a line of credit, or multiple income sources outside of your job that you can fall back on when things get messed up – and at some point they usually do. That's just the nature of things.

Abide By the Golden Rule

The Golden Rule says that you should treat others the way that you would want to be treated. True success is dependent upon this law of reciprocity – to do onto others as you would have them do onto you. People can become wealthy by screwing over others. We all know this. You just need to watch the news and you can see examples of this. This is not success – this is fraud and conning other people. Nothing good will come of that.

Success that you can feel good about when you go to bed at night, or when you look yourself in the mirror, means treating others as you would like to be treated. We discussed earlier the idea of over-delivering for your clients or customers. That is one way that you can implement the Golden Rule in your dealings with others.

Whenever you're struggling with a problem or an ethical dilemma, you simply need to change places with the other person. What would I want them to do for me in this same situation? That can be your moral compass, and makes decision-making much easier. Do the right thing – your reputation is the most valuable thing that you have. The amount of success that you achieve in life will be a direct result of your ability to abide by the Golden Rule.

Be Flexible – Hot dogs or Shrimp Take-out?

I have a friend who is an entrepreneur. She supports her family of four with her small business, and has done so successfully for over twenty years. As with any business owner, her income goes up and down according to how business is going at any point in time. Before going into business for myself, I asked her how she deals with the uncertainty and the ups and down in her income stream.

"We're flexible – we can eat hot dogs when money's tight, and other times, when the money is just flowing in, we can eat shrimp take-out."

Successful people learn to be flexible to make things work out.

Do You Need Help?

Don't let what you cannot do interfere with what you can do. John R. Wooden

No one's good at everything. Some people think that they are, but that's a whole other issue. Being successful means knowing what you're good at, and what your weaknesses are. Some people think that they should work on their weaknesses in order to become successful. In actuality, you'll be far more successful if you play to your strengths and make the most of those. But, hey – what do you do about your weaknesses?

Everyone's different – and your weaknesses are someone else's strengths. What you need to do is discover what your weaknesses are and then find someone else to handle those things. You might decide you want to get a partner so that he or she can handle the things that you aren't very good at. Sometimes, that may be the answer. Another option is to hire someone as a contractor to do the things that you don't do so well. In many cases, hiring a contractor will be a better option because you won't have to be in a partnership with another person. You simply pay them a fee to do what you need him or her to do, and then you move on. You can even hire them regularly if they perform a good service for you. You will maintain the control if you don't enter into a partnership with them. Just make sure if you hire a contractor that you have everything in writing (a contract) so you don't get burned.

Outsourcing

Outsourcing is a great way to do more than you otherwise could on your own. There are many places that you can turn to if you need to outsource some of your tasks. These can be writing business plans, creating a logo, writing articles, or simply just doing administrative assistant-type jobs.

Here's a list of places where you can find individuals that you would pay so you can outsource tasks that you either can't do on your own or things that should be done by someone else. This way, you can handle matters that are more important or can not be outsourced to another person. It's all about making the best use of your time and increasing your overall output.

I've hired people off of Fiverr.com, where you can get people to do things for $5 and up. It's one of my first go-to places. I've also hired contractors off of elance.com to design logos for me. Odesk.com is extremely popular, and you can sometimes find online contractors on Craigslist as well. Other freelance sites include ifreelance, freelancer,and People Per Hour. There are, of course, many more but that should at least get you started.

Think Outside of the Box

Try to think in a creative or original way. If you do things the way that everyone else does, you will get the results that everyone else gets – usually nothing that spectacular. Think outside of the box. Use what you've learned about yourself and your strengths. Is there a way you can use your own individualized abilities to start a new kind of business? Can you use those strengths to somehow generate additional income for yourself and your family? Can you use creative thinking to put you on the road to success? Take some time to think about it – and the possibilities.

Your Differences will Make You a Success

In order to be a success, you must stand out from the crowd. Most people aren't successful – they simply don't go the distance to achieve that. How does one stand out from the crowd? They have to be different! It's a bit ironic that in school, they teach us all the same things and want us all to act the same – to be homogenous. They are trying to raise happy little citizens. In real life, it is your differences that will make all the difference and help you rise above the masses. How are you different than other people? What do you do better than most?

Sometimes, it is easy for us to analyze others, but difficult to analyze ourselves. It may help to ask a friend or relative how they think you are different? Be careful – you might get some interesting replies depending on who you ask! In any case, we want to capitalize on ways that you are different than other people and the things that you might do better than the average person. Those are the things that will propel you on your pathway to a successful future.

Grow and Grow

It's a cliché – do what you've always done, and you'll get what you've always gotten. In addition to educating yourself and learning as many new skills as possible, you need to grow your universe. Expand it. Network with others who can help you along in your journey.

All our dreams can come true if we have the courage to pursue them. Walt Disney

If you expand your universe, good things happen. Give yourself the luxury of dreaming again. Do you even remember what your dreams were? What did you want to do when you were a child? What were your dreams? Did you ever make a list of things you wanted to do in life or with your life? The monotony of every day can sometimes steal our dreams away from us. We get so busy with our jobs and our families that we forget what it is that we really wanted to begin with. Think about it. Don't your dreams deserve a chance?

You will find that life rewards action. The more you do, the more rewards you will eventually see. If you keep to yourself and do little to further yourself and your situation, you will not see the rewards that you would otherwise realize. When all else fails, do something…

Remember that life is not an all or nothing prospect – you can keep your current job and start working on your dreams on the side.

Make Changes

The first step toward success is taken when you refuse to be a captive of the environment in which you first find yourself. Mark Caine

The greatest gift we have in life is our free will – the ability to change our lives for the better…or sometimes worse. Let's aim for BETTER!

Here's a secret: You can change your life! Is your life a mess? Are you in debt? Out of work? Are you depressed? Do you feel lost or just plain stuck? Are you out of shape? Has your road to success diverted off into the ditch? Guess what? You're not alone! It has happened to the best of us. Here's where the challenge comes in. What are you made of? A dead end street is just the place to turn around. And when you get down to nothing, you've got nothing to lose – right?

You can turn it all around. Start making changes. Do you take a bath every day? Try taking a shower. Have you always toyed with the idea of becoming a vegetarian? Give it a try. Don't exercise? Start with doing a thousand jumping jacks a day in your living room. Hate your job? Start looking for a better one. You have the power – and no one else will ever do it for you! Change a little at a time until you get your life back on track. That will be your first step to success. Get up out of the ditch and get back on the road again. You can do it!

Birds of a Feather

Find like-minded people – if there aren't any physically around you, you can find them on the internet. Visit forums for people who are either interested in the same things you are, or who are interested in the things you are interested in doing. Or, even better, fine people who are already doing the things you want to do. Making contacts like this helps, even if you don't consider yourself someone who would like to hang out on forums. It helps to be able to ask a question and get answers from various people who know or who may have more experience in a certain area than you do. You can make friends, and maybe even find someone to do a project with – if you need or are interested in that. As always, beware of those you meet on the internet. Never send anyone money, of course. Do your due diligence to make sure you know who you're dealing with. While you can make contact with many great people via the Internet, scammers are prevalent! Stay safe.

Sacrifice Something

Whenever you see a successful person you only see the public glories, never the private sacrifices to reach them. **Vaibhav Shah**

You have to be willing to sacrifice. Great athletes sacrifice large amounts of time practicing and honing their particular sport. Entrepreneurs sacrifice large blocks of personal time to grow their own businesses and bring their ideas to fruition. Professionals like doctors sacrifice many hours in schooling and training. Sometimes, ideas require one to sacrifice start-up funds to get things going. Most things that lead to success require a sacrifice of time (researching, training, schooling) or funds, and sometimes both.

My preference is always to sacrifice time instead of money, whenever possible. However, everyone's situation is different. The point here is, be prepared to sacrifice something – but do your research, your due diligence, and think it through first. Smart sacrifice is the key.

Perhaps No One Can Tell You How to Do It

We are all walking our own path in life. No one has the same life experience that you do. Search the world over looking for an exact clone of you and all of your experiences, good and bad, in this world. You will not find such a person. Your dream may differ greatly from anyone else's dream. It may very well be that you have to figure it out for yourself. Will you succeed the first time you try something? Probably not....get that in your brain right now and you won't be afraid of failure.

Let's think this through.

> **What do you want to do?** This could be start a business, find a way to make money online, what is your dream? What's the goal? What are we going for here?
>
> **Research the hell out of it.** Look online, investigate how others did the same thing or a similar feat, what would you need to do, what are the legalities, what are the first steps, where can you get more information? What would achieving your goal entail? What would it look like?
>
> **Make one small step.** Whether it's more research, contacting someone who knows more about it than you do, registering your new business name....you have to start somewhere.
>
> **Build upon that first small step.** What is your next logical step? Come up with a plan. What will you do and in what order.
>
> **Proceed until you Succeed.** Keep going – move forward, build a little at a time, make mistakes, fix the mistakes, change course, keep working it out. That is how success is built.

Think Big!

Once your find a small success, you need to think how you can grow that success exponentially. It may take time to find a way to make even a small success. But, when you do, don't give up then! Your next step is to think of a way to expand that success. Do you need to hire a contractor to do some of the work for you so you can double your output? Do you need to hire several contractors to really maximize the amount of money you are currently making? Run the numbers. Try different things. If you stop with a small success or win, you'll never know just how successful you can really become.

Are you limiting your own success without even knowing it? I once heard it said that "you will never make one cent more than you believe you are capable of making." This actually makes a lot of sense when you think about it. Do you think you're capable of making $30,000 a year? Do you think you can make more? Do you think you can make $100,000 a year? What about $300,000? What about $500,000? It may be that you are limiting yourself in your own mind.

Sometimes we get complacent. Maybe things are going all right. You're paying the bills, you have a little extra money available. You're going on day after day. If you're satisfied with this, you're not going to try harder. You're not going to try for more. Take some time to think about it. Have you become too complacent in your life? If you want more success, you have to want more. You have to really want more. Now, what are you going to do about it?

80/20 Pareto Principle

No book about success would be complete without discussing the Pareto Principle, which many successful entrepreneurs use to supersize their success. The Pareto Principle says that in many circumstances, including business, 20% is vital while 80% is trivial. So, a small business owner may find that 80% of his sales revenue comes from just 20% of his best customers. By using this principle, it is often possible to change things in a business so that you can minimize or get rid of customers or activities that cause the most problems and/or bring in the least revenue.

So, it may be in your best interest to concentrate on giving the best service and attention to the 20% of your customers that bring in 80% of your revenue and ignore the rest. Focusing your attention on finding other "best customers" would be time better spent than dealing with small-time customers who are needy and bring in only a small amount of money. The ultimate result would be less work, less frustration, and more money. It's all a part of working smarter. You only have so many hours in a day. Figure out which of your activities bring in the most income, and spend more time on those activities. Scrap the things that are just wasting your time (like constantly checking email or Facebook). It seems like common sense, but sometimes in our pursuit of success, we fail to see the obvious.

Being Small Makes You Flexible

Being small isn't always a disadvantage. As an individual instead of a large company, you are much more flexible as you move towards success. You can make all the decisions – that means decisions can be made very quickly. Let's say you decide to become an independent publisher and books on unicorns become very popular. You can make the decision immediately to begin working on a book on that subject. It's fast. You can react quickly to the marketplace, while other large companies are bound and wound up in red tape. How can being lean and mean propel you along the road to success? Take advantage of the advantages that you have. Being small and flexible is one of them.

Confidence is Not Something – It's Everything

Confidence is everything – whether you're going to a job interview or approaching someone with a business proposal. You must exude confidence, even if you feel like you're faking it. Why would someone hire you for a job if you don't act confident in your ability to be hired for it? Why would anyone accept a business proposal from you if they don't feel you are confident in your own abilities? The answer is simple; they won't. You need to believe in yourself if you're ever going to expect anyone else to believe in you.

Dress nicely, and speak with confidence. Act like a professional. If you have doubts in yourself, others will easily pick up on those doubts. We can easily read the body language of other people. You will be selling yourself short in all of your endeavors if you don't enter into them with a self-assured demeanor. To be successful, you first need to get the chance to start. Without confidence, it'll be over before you even get started. Be confident!

Personality Plus

Are you a nice person? Are people naturally drawn to you? Most people come across well if they are being their genuine selves. The more authentic they are, the more people will pick up on that authenticity. They will trust you and what you are saying.

Success often requires becoming involved with others to some extent, whether they be partners, investors, clients or customers. Personality, or more specifically, having a pleasing personality, is invaluable in your pursuit of success. If people like you, they will want to help you. If they don't, then they most certainly won't.

Influencing others is crucial to success. Making others like you will have the greatest impact on your ability to influence them. Think of the most successful leaders in history (JFK, Martin Luther King) – how would their success have been handicapped if they weren't as well-liked, and therefore influential?

Here's a list of personality traits that people find appealing:

Accountable, Alert, Assertive, Authentic, Compassionate, Creative, Determined, Disciplined, Ethical, Happy, Honorable, Innovative, Joyful, Listener, Optimistic, Poised, Peaceful, Practical, Problem-Solver, Poised, Reliable, Self-Confident, Humorous, Sincere, Spontaneous, Trusting, Willing, Versatile, Ambitious, Candid, Charismatic, Committed, Considerate, Cooperative, Curious, Diplomatic, Dynamic, Efficient, Energetic, Excited, Fair, Flexible, Generous, Hard-working, Independent, Integrity, Knowledgeable, Interested, Organized,

Loyal, Polite, Resourceful, Stable, Supportive, Trustworthy, Enthusiastic, Wise, Empathetic, Adventurous, Consistent, Connected, Communicative, Easy-going, Friendly, Honest, Gratitude, Open-Minded, Patient, Proactive, Punctual, Responsible, Self-reliant, Strong, Tactful, Truthful.

There are obviously many more – but I'm sure you get the idea. You shouldn't try to be something you're not, but we all have room for improvement and growth. Consider how your dealings with others could be improved by working on just a few of these. Could you become more punctual or better with your time management? Could you better express gratitude to those you interact with? Many times, a simple smile can make you enormously more likeable and approachable. The better you are able to get this personality thing perfected, the more successful you will be in life.

Motivation

Be Miserable. Or Motivate Yourself. Whatever has to be done, it's your choice. Wayne Dyer

People often say that motivation doesn't last. Well, neither does bathing - that's why we recommend it daily. Zig Ziglar

What exactly is motivation anyway? Enthusiasm, drive, ambition, initiative, determination, and enterprise. I'm not sure anyone can teach or learn motivation. It is the drive within. Do you have the determination and desire to achieve success? I know you have an interest in it, because you're reading this book. But, do you have the motivation? It's probably only a question that you can answer for yourself.

True motivation means that you keep on going, even when the going is tough. You don't stop, even when things get screwed up. You get up each and every day and do something to push yourself along your path to success. When things go badly, you make adjustments and move on. In fact, you think positively, but you know everything is not always going to be smooth sailing. That's just life. Stay determined, for success is not possible without it.

Faith...Or Knowing That You Can and Will Succeed

To accomplish great things, we must not only act, but also dream, not only plan, but also believe. Anatole France

The ones who are crazy enough to think they can change the world, are the ones that do. Anonymous

Nothing beats knowing that you can and will succeed. Belief is a very powerful thing, no matter how intangible it may seem. Do you truly believe you can become a success? Do you have faith in your ability to do the things you need to do in order to achieve success in your life? Unfortunately, I don't believe you can become a success unless you believe it is a possibility.

We've worked on making success a concrete notion for you. I asked you to define success for yourself and consider creating a vision board of success for you to refer to – in order to keep the idea of success and what it entails in the forefront of your mind. Success must seem as real to you as a loaf of bread sitting on your kitchen counter. You can see it, you can taste it, and you know what it will take to get it. The more success seems real to you, the easier it is to believe in the possibility of actually reaching it. Have faith in your ability to become successful.

If It Works, Do More of It

Again, this seems relatively common-sense in nature. However, you'd be surprised how many times people tell me about something they did that was incredible successful, and then they went on to try a bunch of different things that were complete failures. They can't seem to find anything that was as successful as that one thing. They try and try but success eludes them.

My first question is: Why did they switch gears? They found a method that was successful – a method that worked. Why did they change course and go on a wild goose chase after something else? While I encourage people to try different things, if you find a successful method then you should stick with it if possible. Stay with it until you've taken advantage of all of the possibilities it has, and then expand into other ideas.

I think sometimes people say they want success, but really they're afraid of it. Perhaps it's some childhood memory of their father saying "rich people are cheats." I don't pretend to understand the psychology behind it, but I think that some people believe that bad things will happen if they become successful. Some people don't want the responsibility. I've actually met people who told me they wouldn't want the responsibility of a higher level job or more money. Perhaps these are the reasons that people switch gears once they find a way to be successful.

In any case, if you find success in one of your endeavors – keep doing it. Figure out how you can do more of it, or how you can expand it. That small success just may be your ticket to one huge success someday down the road.

Enjoy the Journey

Failure is the condiment that gives success its flavor. Truman Capote

The road to success can be hard and long. I tried for years, and many different things, before I was able to find a way to have the life I have today – the life that I love. There were failures along the way, times when I was laid off and felt like the rug had been pulled out right from under me. I moved on, I found another way – a better way. The best advice I can give to you is to enjoy the journey. You can't truly appreciate real success without first knowing failure.

You actually learn much more from your failures than you

do from your successes. You learn what not to do, you learn what doesn't work. You look at the mistakes you made, and hopefully learn from those mistakes. Did you fail to plan properly? Did you forget to have a back-up plan in place? Did you simply give up when times got tough? Did you then, eventually, pull yourself back together and get back up?

What did you learn about yourself from your failures? Chances are, you learned you are far tougher and more resilient than you ever realized. You don't have to love your failures – who does? But it's important to take them for what they are. Failures are learning opportunities in disguise. The more you fail, the more you learn. It is all of that learning, all of those lessons born of failure, that will eventually lead you to where you want to go.

Enjoy the journey. Someday, you may even look back and laugh at all of those misadventures that occurred along the way to your success. Have an interesting journey – it will be unlike anyone else's. Make it your own, and do the things you want to do. Stay motivated, confident in the knowledge that the victory will one day be yours.

More Inspirational Quotes and Philosophies

Try not to become a person of success, but rather a person of value. Albert Einstein

I have not failed. I've just found 10,000 ways that won't work. Thomas Edison

If you're going through hell, keep going. Winston Churchill

A successful man is one who can lay a firm foundation with the bricks others have thrown at him. David Brinkley

The whole secret of a successful life is to find out what is one's destiny to do, and then do it. Henry Ford

Don't be afraid to give up the good and go for the great. John D. Rockefeller

You measure the size of the accomplishment by the obstacles you had to overcome to reach your goals. Booker T. Washington

You must expect great things of yourself before you can do them. Michael Jordan

There is no chance, no destiny, no fate, that can hinder or control the firm resolve of a determined soul. Ella Wheeler Wilcox

Success is...knowing your purpose in life, growing to reach your maximum potential, and sowing seeds that benefit others. John C. Maxwell

Additional Resources: Popular Books About Success

Outliers: The Story of Success by Malcolm Gladwell

Think and Grow Rich by Napoleon Hill

The Seven Habits of Highly Effective People by Stephen Covey

How to Win Friends and Influence People by Dale Carnegie

The Success Principles: How to Get from Where You Are to Where You Want to Be by Jack Canfield

Drive: The Surprising Truth About What Motivates Us by Daniel Pink

Rich Dad, Poor Dad by Robert Kiyosaki

The Magic of Thinking Big by David Schwartz

The Richest Man in Babylon by George Clason

Conclusion

It seems as though we've come to the end of our journey here. We've gone over a lot of information, so perhaps a review would be helpful.

First, we defined success – what does success mean to you? We've discussed writing down your goals and creating a vision board to remind you daily of the task at hand.

You have to be willing to work, to ask others when you want to collaborate, and to put your work out there. If you've fallen, you must pull yourself back up and start on your new path to success. Focus, control your time, get organized, and save up some money. Do your research, and be willing to learn and try new things. Read some of the books that I've listed above for your convenience. Do something for yourself aside from your regular job. Over-deliver for your clients, and add value whenever possible. Make sure to have a back-up plan.

Get help or outsource if you need to. Be flexible while pursuing your success ventures. Do unto others as you would have them do unto you. Be creative and think outside of the box when developing your ideas and plans. Capitalize on the things that make you different than others. Grow, make changes, and network with other like-minded individuals. Be willing to sacrifice.

Think big while realizing that being small right now makes you more flexible. Be confident, motivated, and most importantly, have faith in knowing that you can and will succeed. When you find a little success, make sure you figure out how to maximize it. And, of course, enjoy your journey along the way.

Success does not come easily. It comes through hard work. No two people have the same path to success. We are all on individualized journeys. Although we can develop the philosophies of others who have been successful before us, we ultimately must find our own way. Work, research, stay motivated, try different things, make adjustments to your plan, and most importantly, keep going. Enjoy yourself as you grow and learn. It won't be easy – but then again, nothing good ever is.

Wishing you every success in life, my friend...

Afterword

If you've enjoyed this book, please take a minute to leave a review on Amazon so that other people will take the opportunity to learn more about how to make a living online. I truly believe we can revive our economy through entrepreneurship - people starting their own businesses and not relying on big business for jobs.